SHELL CRAFT

Virginie Fowler Elbert

PHOTOGRAPHS BY THE AUTHOR
DRAWINGS BY LORETTA TREZZO

DOVER PUBLICATIONS, INC.
New York

Copyright

Published in Canada by General Publishing Company, Ltd., 30 Lesmill Road, Don Mills, Toronto, Ontario.
Published in the United Kingdom by Constable and Company, Ltd., 3 The Lanchesters, 162–164 Fulham Palace Road, London W6 9ER.

Bibliographical Note

This Dover edition, first published in 1993, is a republication of *Shell Craft*, originally published by Bobbs-Merrill, Indianapolis/New York, in 1977. The color plates in the original edition have been omitted and the section "Sources for Supplies" has been updated for this edition.

.

Library of Congress Cataloging-in-Publication Data

Fowler, Virginie, 1916–
    Shell craft / Virginie Fowler Elbert ; photographs by the author ; drawings by Loretta Trezzo.
        p.   cm.
    Revised reprint. Originally published: Indianapolis ; New York : Bobbs-Merrill, 1977.
    Includes bibliographical references and index.
    ISBN 0-486-27730-5
    1. Shellcraft.   I. Title.
TT862.F68   1993
745.55—dc20   93-28187
                                                          CIP

Manufactured in the United States of America
Dover Publications, Inc., 31 East 2nd Street, Mineola, N.Y. 11501

ACKNOWLEDGMENTS

To Dr. William K. Emerson of the American Museum of Natural History, New York City, for identifying the orange banded rare color form of *Oliva reticularis* described by Koester in 1866, which I found in St. Lucia, West Indies, in October 1975.

To Suzanne Elbert Rothwell, whose beautiful finished designs are shown in Figs. 16, 30, 34, 48 and 64.

To the Metropolitan Museum of Art in New York City, for their kind permission to use the following photographs: Fig. 2, Contribution from Henry Walters and the Rogers Fund, 1916. (16.1.5); Fig. 3, Bequest of Benjamin Altman, 1913. (14.40.667); Fig. 4, Rogers Fund, 1906. (06.1021.261); Fig. 5, Gift of Carlton Macy, 1934. (34.165.54ab). (All rights reserved, The Metropolitan Museum of Art).

And a special thanks to George Parsons who, a number of years ago, gave me the Ohio River "pearl button" shell (Fig. 7), his remembrance of his boyhood on the River.

Contents

SHELL CRAFT

Shells as Decorative Objects

GATHERING SHELLS is part of summer for many of us—or we bring them back from a relaxed winter vacation on a tropical beach. When a single shell is put on a stand it recaptures the mood of that other time and place. Then what? A bag of shells brought back in triumph, but now sitting on a closet shelf. Or, beautiful shells admired in a shell shop window—but what can one do with them? Or, you may have admired expensive gift items made of shells and wondered how they are made.

Wonder no more. Here you'll find directions for casting shell designs in clear, sparkling plastic, or decorating boxes and mirrors that are tongue-in-cheek Victorian, or making fun containers of clay. The craft possibilities are endless, and each chapter leads you, with clear directions, into the handling of the materials, with enough detailed designs to begin with before starting off on your own projects. Jewelry, printed paper and cloth, clever things for adornment, decorative objects that are practical in an elegant way and things that are just made to look at and enjoy, because shells are the source of fascinating designs and the main material for a number of amusing decorative crafts. All these modern shell projects are described in simple step-by-step procedures complete with identifying shell photographs and drawings of the finished designs.

Where can you buy shells if you haven't been to a beach lately? They are available for craft projects at craft or shell shops or in department stores. They can be ordered by catalog from mail order companies specializing in shells and minerals. Check the back of this book for names and addresses, or look in the Yellow Pages of the telephone book under Shells-Marine or Craft or Art Supplies. But best of all is beachcombing—especially in warm southern waters off the coasts of Florida and

Sanibel Island, then along the Gulf Coast and down into Puerto Rico and the West Indian islands. In the West, along the Pacific Coast, then out to the islands—wherever there is ocean water you'll find shells.

And as you collect shells it will seem incredible that the soft, flabby clam- and snail-like bodies could manufacture such hard, complicated and colorful outer coverings from the cold sea water—all without the clay, chemicals and intense heat we need to produce fine glazed porcelain. Just the color forms and slight variations within one genus are amazing. For instance, the Scallop Shell of the northern Atlantic beaches is a mottled gray or dull black, but as one goes further south the color changes into bright orange, lemon yellow or a mottled calico pattern that includes brown, ivory, rust and orange. In the southern waters, knobs and bumps are added to form the Lion's Paw. Flat fan shapes in a sunray pattern of lavender and rust turn up on Florida and West Indian beaches. In the Pacific some species are bright purple or pure, pure white. This is only one of the infinite variety of forms which change from genus to genus. With such incredible shapes it is no wonder that shells have never gone out of fashion, and at times have reached the peak of collector mania as they were auctioned for high prices and became precious objects in jewel-like cabinets.

Shells have been an ever-recurring theme in art and crafts since ancient times. Probably because so many early civilizations bordered the Mediterranean Sea it was natural for shells to be used as motifs by artists and craftspeople. In Egyptian tombs many shell-inspired designs have been found, including the girdle shown in Fig. 2, which is from the XII Dynasty. It belonged to Princess Sat-hathor-iunut, and was made of cowrie shapes cast in gold and linked together with rhomboid-shaped beads of gold, carnelian and green feldspar—a luxurious jewel that could be worn today as a belt or neck chain.

Other popular shells of the Mediterranean are Scallop and Cockle Shells, the ever-recurring art themes in this area through the centuries. They turn up in paintings, in pottery, in jeweled objects and as architectural motifs. Both shells have been known as the Pilgrim's Shell, proving as it were, that the traveler had reached a holy shrine on the shores of the Mediterranean Sea. This was true whether he traveled the road from Paris through France to Rome, bringing back the honored Coquille St. Jacques (a name now associated with scallops cooked with a sauce and served in a shell), or to Spain in the ninth to twelfth centuries where the Cockle Shell was the symbol of a pilgrimage to Santiago de Compostela where a star had shone over St. James's body. Even as late as the middle of the nineteenth century, Charles Dickens wrote in his "Pictures from

14

Fig. 1. *An assortment of Florida and West Indian Scallop Shells (Pecten), including (top center) a Lion's Paw (Pecten nodosus), Fan Shell (Pecten ziczac) and a Calico Scallop (Pecten gibbus).*

Fig. 2. *An Egyptian girdle of gold cowries and beads of gold, carnelian and green feldspar belonged to Princess Sat-hathor-iunut of the XII dynasty.*

Italy" of the pilgrims "who are now repairing to their own homes again—each with his scallop shell and staff . . ."

In this brief chapter it is impossible to list and show all the art objects that have come down to us, as in Italy alone shells were used as formal architectural decorations over doorways and on walls, in floor mosaics covered with dolphins, crabs and shells with the merman Triton blowing on his twisted shell—all done in small black tiles against white—a cool sea-like floor to take one through the hot summer days. The goldsmiths, too, were busy with shell designs of enamel and gold in the form of elaborate pendants to hang around the neck on a gold chain. And there is the famous Rospigliosi cup, which is one of the most elegant designs of the Renaissance in gold and enamel, pearls and jewels, with its wide gold Scallop Shell balanced on the back of a turtle (Fig. 3).

When shell designs worked their way westward into England, they again adorned houses and furniture as part of the English admiration for classical things. There is a strong resemblance between the shell-decorated vase of early Mediterranean times (Fig. 4), and the Staffordshire teapot made around 1745, shown in Fig. 5.

FIG. 3. *Cup, formerly known as the Rospigliosi Cup. Gold, enamel, pearls.*

FIG. 4. *A vase in the shape of a shell of either Greek or Roman origin which dates back to 300–200 B.C.*

FIG. 5.   A Staffordshire teapot of salt-glazed stoneware
made around 1745 in England.

Shells were also part of the religious experience of many of the African and Pacific island cultures whose monumental wood carvings and elaborate ceremonial robes had small Cowrie Shells worked into their elaborate designs. They were symbols used in puberty rites, as well as good luck fetishes to place on the prows of South Pacific canoes to ward off evil spirits (Fig. 6).

In our own country the small polished beads on the heavy wampum belts of the American Indians were made from Clam and Whelk Shells, and when the settlers invaded the Indian's world an exchange value was established between the European coins and wampum beads which were the Indian's coinage.

Some of the wampum may have been made from fresh-water mussels, clams or oysters—the names seem to have been interchangeable—which were found in large quantities in the Ohio and Mississippi rivers. These were the large six-inches-across shells of the Midwest, and *were* is the right verb, as they were fished out in the early part of this century in the

FIG. 6. *The Pacific Ocean white Cowrie Shell lined with glowing rust-brown is 3½ inches long.*

FIG. 7. *A three-ridge fresh-water pearly Oyster Shell taken from the Ohio River in 1909, showing the core-drilled holes for buttons.*

greedy quest for shells for pearl buttons. Fig. 7 shows a punched-out shell, a reminder of a forgotten industry.

With all the advantages of these past designs, plus all the new materials available to us—clear plastics for molding and embedding, quick baking clays for oven temperatures that are kind to shells, easy printing processes for fabrics—we can develop new approaches to this old and satisfying craft. Look in old books for shell drawings, some of them hand-colored as those in G. B. Sowerby's *Popular British Conchology* (see the reproduction of one plate in Fig. 8), or in modern handbooks or encyclopedias for photographs to be used as the basis of designs. Gather your seashells around you and settle down to create new settings for your treasures which are part of the natural life of the seashore, of summer and of the tropics.

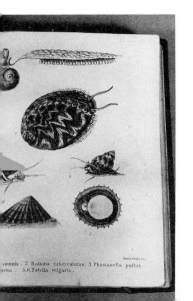

FIG. 8. *A hand-colored plate from George Brettingham Sowerby's* Popular British Conchology *published in London, 1854.*

18

PART I

SHELLS
FOR
REAL

1

How to Make Displays for Your Shells

SHELLS ARE COLLECTED for their beauty and displayed as art objects. Collecting is a pure treasure hunt as one walks along beaches, clambers over rocks, wades in the shallows at low tide—always looking for the unusual shell, for a flash of color, a different shape. And then, the quick scooping up of the shell from sand or water—the excitement and triumph of a new possession. The loot depends on the beach location, the time of year and the tide, and each expedition becomes a new experience.

We have shelled up and down the ocean coasts, along the Gulf of Mexico and on the beaches and coral reefs of Puerto Rico and St. Lucia. Other shells have been collected by happenstance. While photographing wild flowers on a hillside near Volterra in Italy, we saw a piece of a fossil shell half buried in the yellow dirt. On that same trip, after spending a day looking at the mosaics and churches in Ravenna, we went out to the shore area of the Adriatic to eat at one of the seafood restaurants. But first we kicked off our shoes and scooped up treasures from the flat, dark sand, thinly covered with water. One of the shells was a Pelican's Foot (*Apporhais pespelicani*).

Another haul was a pure fluke as we waited for the guide to collect enough people for the tour through the Abbey at Fontevraud in France. I was boredly kicking at the gravel and dirt of the parking lot, when I saw a

FIG. 9. *A Pelican's Foot from Ravenna, a piece of fossil shell from Volterra and a shell from the parking area of the Abbey at Fontevraud.*

sharp point gleaming with mother-of-pearl. A few more sharp kicks brought up a South Seas shell, then several others surfaced. Undoubtedly, the gravel and sand was ballast brought back by ship from a French possession and the shells came along for the ride. They were all in good shape and were brought home to add to our collection.

Another great collecting spot at any time of the year is the counter of a shell shop. Here are shells from all over the world and you can pick and choose among the many exotic varieties. Do you like Cone Shells, Cowries, Murexes or Scallop Shells? Look for them on counters and shelves.

What do you do if you live far from an ocean shore and there are no shell shops nearby? Do not despair. Mail order houses specializing in shells will send catalogs on request, and you can order both present-day shells and fossil shells millions of years old. Many of the catalogs are illustrated with pages of photographs, so that you can see what type of shell you are ordering. There are shells for single display and others for decorating projects.

There are many types and different shapes, surface designs and colors in each family of shells, each with its own name. A field guide book will help you identify your haul and separate the *Gastropoda* from the *Pelecypoda*. A list of helpful books is on page 277.

Many shells are known by their common name but the Latin name is the true identification as a common name can change from area to area. For this reason many catalogs and handbooks list the shells by their Latin names. The beginning beachcomber often lumps all large, flat shells as "clams," but you'll find that a clam is not a clam. Try to find a listing in a handbook under "Clam"—you'll find Surf Clam (*Spisula solidissima*), or Quahog (*Venus mercenaria*); each belongs to a different genus, even though to the untutored eye they might look somewhat alike. And there are many other similar shapes with different common names and Latin names.

No matter how you acquire your shells you will soon find that you want to display them, to show off their strange and beautiful shapes to the best advantage. You will also want to clean and restore their colors so they will look as they did when you snatched them from the water, all glistening and gleaming.

CLEANING AND PREPARING SHELLS

Tools and Materials

Very few tools are needed and they are of the simplest—both materials and tools are part of a standard household.

A *nutpick, metal skewer* or *dental scraper* for cleaning away any excess pieces of lime adhering to the shell surfaces. A *wire brush* is very useful in removing the most stubborn lime deposits.

To scrape out any leftover pieces of snail from the Gastropods, use a piece of *thin wire*, a *hairpin*, a *long pin*, or an *opened paper clip*.

The other shell cleaners are a household *chlorine bleach* for boiling out the shells, *rubbing alcohol* to drop into the center of the snail type to destroy any odor-causing material still left in the point. *Baby oil* or *mineral oil* to bring out shell color after cleaning. A soft *water-color brush* to apply the oil.

And finally, *stick-on labels* on which to identify your shells.

FIG. 10. *Tools for cleaning shells include a safety pin, two dental scrapers, an eyedropper, a fine wire dental tool, skewer, an open paper clip, plus a wire brush, baby oil and rubbing alcohol.*

Preparing the Shells

When you get home from the beach and look at your shells, you'll be disappointed. What has happened to their bright, fresh colors? They now seem drab, the colors are faded and grayish, and bits of barnacle or other limey encrustations are sticking to the surfaces. The only shells that do not seem to have suffered a land change are the Cowries and Olive Shells with their hard, porcelain-like surfaces. It was the water that kept the shells looking so bright, and bringing them back to their original colors is a two-step process.

The first step seems to be a paradox. The shells are put into a pot and covered with cold water. Chlorine bleach is added in the proportion of two tablespoons of bleach to one cup of water, and the whole lot is brought to a boil, then simmered for four or five minutes. While chlorine is thought of as a powerful bleach, it also loosens lime substances and other discolorations that stick to the surface of shells, and as their color is built into their structure, it is not affected by the bleach. Remove from the water, rinse off in hot to warm water.

Household lye, for instance the Red Devil brand, in the proportion of one-quarter pound or a bit less to one quart of *cold* water, is also a good overnight soaking medium for loosening or removing lime deposits which often cover the bright surface of a shell. Follow the manufacturer's directions for the containers you use for soaking—usually china or glass. While this method, as well as the hot Clorox solution, may not completely remove all blemishes, it does loosen the toughest materials, making it easier to scrape them off with a metal tool. Be sure to wear rubber gloves when handling the shells after they have soaked in lye. Rinse off the shells in cold, running water, making sure that the insides of the snail-like types are very well flushed with clear water.

Scrape off any remaining bits of lime with a nutpick, skewer or dental tool. (If you are going in for shell collecting, this latter tool is invaluable, so ask your dentist for discarded scrapers.) Give the shells a final rinsing in lukewarm water and let dry on paper towels.

If a Snail Shell is fresh, clean it out after boiling. First, remove the cover over the opening—the *operculum*—which also can be used in shell projects. Then hook a piece of wire into the snail, and pull very slowly but steadily until you have pulled it completely out of the shell. There may still be a small amount of meat left in the point, so add a few drops of rubbing alcohol and wait a few days. Rinse out, and all should be well.

The second step is to coat each shell lightly with baby or mineral oil,

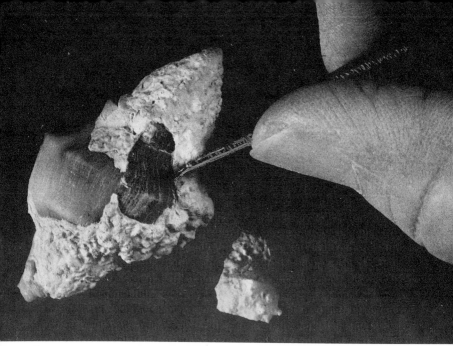

FIG. 11.   *A piece of lime deposit has just been chipped off a shell.*

FIG. 12.   *Photograph shows heavily encrusted shells and the clean shell that is under the lime coating.*

applying it with a soft water-color brush. Let the oil soak in overnight, and then wipe off any excess with a soft cloth or well-crumpled paper towel. Your shells will now be bright and fresh colored. Of course, if they were very old and sun-bleached on the beach, they will be improved but not perfect. So, when you are gathering shells, be strong-willed and discard all but the best before you leave the beach.

Now, identify your shells by comparing them to the photographs and descriptions in a good field guide. Then make a record by placing a small identifying number on your shell and keeping the name and location and date found in a notebook.

DISPLAYING SHELLS

There are a number of ways to display shells as art objects. Five different ways will be described in this chapter, ranging from single shells to a small collection. Adapting these basic approaches, you will be able to use other available containers. So look over your collection and, depending on how many shells you have, decide which is the best way to show them off.

Tools and Materials

Household tools are used throughout this section. Specific tools may vary depending on the project but the most frequently used are: *hammer, screwdriver, rasp, metal* and *wood files, saw, metal cutter, metal scriber, paint brushes* and *scissors.*

Also, the materials depend on the project. First, and most important—*shells.* Then *paint, shellac, felt, velvet* or other *fabrics, nails, screws, wire, metal furniture decorations, epoxy cement* and *household white glue.*

METAL DISPLAY STAND

Manufactured holders are sold in a few standard sizes. If you make your own, you can adapt the size and the length of the prongs and the height of the stand to your own shell, creating a custom display. The following low stand made of brass or brass-colored wire can be adapted to any size shell by changing its overall size and the thickness of the wire.

Tools and Materials

Pliers, wire cutter, metal file, metal scriber and ruler.

Lengths of brass wire, 3/16 to ¼ inch thick and either round or square, can be bought at a craft or hobby shop, or particularly at a model railroad supply store where various thicknesses are sold in 30-inch lengths. You should not buy wire on a spool as this will have kinks that are very hard to smooth out. Gold-colored wire hangers from the dry cleaner are very handy as the metal is soft and bends easily. As this stand is not heat-soldered, you will need epoxy cement and fine wire for wrapping. To gauge the amount of wire needed, rough measurements are made with heavy cord, approximately the thickness of the final brass wire. Bonnet Shell or any other shell.

Steps

1. A Bonnet Shell (*Cypraecasis rufa*) from the Pacific Ocean is 3⅜ inches long, approximately 2 inches high and 2¼ inches wide. Clean and prepare the shell, if necessary.

2. Cut square brass wire or a wire hanger into the following four lengths: 5 inches and 4⅝ inches for the top support; 6 inches and 7½ inches for the lower support or legs. These measurements are approximate, as there will be inequalities in bending the wire and you will have to snip and file off a bit—especially to level the legs. Always err on the side of too much wire rather than too little.

3. Measure and cut cord the same lengths as the four pieces of wire. Bring the 5-inch cord under the shell lengthwise, and a bit up each side. Mark the bending areas with a felt-tipped pen. Repeat around the middle with the 4⅝-inch cord. *Important reminder. If you are working with a shell of a different size, make your first measurements with the cord, then cut the metal wire.*

4. Lay the pieces of cord alongside the matching pieces of wire and, using two pliers—one to hold the wire steady, the other to bend the wire—curve each end upward. Protect the wire from plier marks with several folds of paper toweling or a small piece of an old leather glove. The lengthwise wire should turn up as far as the point of the shell on one end, and just to the top of the canal opening at the other. The prongs for the center width support should be slightly unequal in height. The "back" will be slightly higher to keep the shell from rolling over, and the "front" shorter to display the outside markings of the lip to the best advantage.

5. Center the two wires—longest on the bottom—and hold firmly while you mark the center crossing with a scriber, a sharp nail or skewer. File a rectangle between the markings on the *top* of the longest wire, halfway down the thickness of the wire. File a rectangle on the *bottom* of the shorter wire between the marks. File halfway through the wire. Place

the wires together and check for fit. They will nestle together, leaving the joint almost level.

6. Repeat the measuring, bending, marking and filing with the two other wires which form the legs of the stand.

7. Check the leg supports to see if they are even. This is easy to do as the fitting together of the wires in the center will hold things steady. File off any excess metal, then smooth and flatten the bottom of each leg. The wires should fit tightly together at the middle. If not, continue to adjust the bottom of the legs with a file.

8. Wipe out the two hollows with rubbing alcohol to clean them of any grease and metal filings. Mix a small amount of epoxy cement. Fill each hollow and put the two leg supports together. Wipe off excess epoxy. Hold tightly with an X crossing of fine wire. Let stand for 24 hours until dry, then cut away holding wire. (For epoxy cement see page 43.)

9. Repeat the process with the top supports or the "shell cradle," checking the length of the wires holding the shell. Make final adjustments of the ends and the curve of the supports. File ends smooth. Add epoxy, hold with fine wire for 24 hours.

10. Cover top and bottom of each joining area with a thin coat of epoxy to insure a good hold. Let dry for another 24 hours.

11. With the file, slightly flatten the areas where the top and bottom supports will be joined to give a better holding area. Put the top cradle on the bottom leg support, coating the joining areas with epoxy cement. Wrap with an X of fine, gold-colored wire, as this will stay on after the epoxy has hardened. Wait for 24 hours before touching the stand.

12. Wrap a few extra turns of wire at the joint. Cover the fine wire and the main heavy wire joint with a thin coat of epoxy and let dry thoroughly. Test all joints for their sturdiness. If you have any doubts, add another thin layer of epoxy and let dry.

13. Now, put your shell in its display holder and place on a table, the mantelpiece or in a bookshelf display area—and admire your handiwork. Your beautiful shell seems to float in space and can be seen from all sides.

FIG. 13. *A Bonnet Shell* (Cypraecasis rufa).

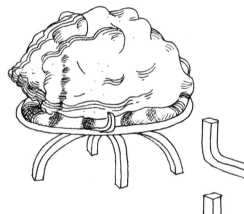

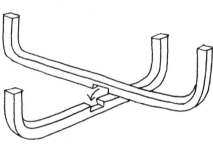

FIG. 14. *Finished shell stand with detail of the center joining of the wires.*

29

A SHADOW BOX

Simple shadow box displays can be made from commercial jewelers' display trays. These are usually oblong, black-painted wood, with a removable cardboard liner which is covered with either black or dark blue velvet. A very handy size is 8¼ x 15 inches, with 1-inch-high sides made of ¼-inch-thick wood.

If you cannot find a tray with a plain insert—only one with a slotted insert for rings—make your own. Cut a sheet of packing case cardboard to size, and cover it with velvet, mitering the corners on the back. Hold the material in place with white glue.

Shells are fastened to the lining with fine wire. Once they are in position the lining is attached to the tray with white glue or epoxy cement and hung on the wall.

Tools and Materials

A thin punch awl for making holes, or a very heavy carpet or sail-maker's needle. A pair of pliers for tightening the wires. A wire cutter or heavy scissors.

Materials include a display tray, velvet and cardboard if needed, fine wire, epoxy cement and shells.

Steps

1. If your shells are beach-gathered, clean and prepare them first.
2. Make a mock-up of your design on a sheet of paper the size of the inside dimensions of your tray. Move the shells around until you have a pleasing arrangement. The one in the photograph contains fossil shells (of the Pliocene period) we gathered in the Lake Okeechobee area of Florida.
3. Lightly trace the outline of each shell with pencil.
4. Each shell is held in place with a length of fine wire. Sometimes the wire goes across its widest part, or is looped at an angle just below the swelling. Then the wire is either brought around and underneath the shell and through the backing, or just brought to the edges of the shell before going through the background material. In any case, always remember that your frame is going to be hung on the wall or stood upright as a display piece, so the shells have to be supported in such a way that they will not fall out of the wires.
5. Mark each shell outline on your pattern with two pencil dots in the places where you think the wire should be pulled through the backing.
6. Following your pattern and starting with the upper left hand

Fig. 15. *Fossil shells of the Pliocene period, gathered by the author in the Lake Okeechobee area of Florida.*

corner, punch two holes through the backing. Feed the point of the wire through one hole from the back. Put the shell down on the velvet covering and bring the wire over it, then through the other hole. Clip off the wire, leaving about one inch at each end. In tightening the wire you will wish that you had four hands until you get used to the procedure. Holding the backing at a slanting, upright angle, press the shell against the background. With the other hand, tighten the wire by twisting with the pliers. The shell-holding hand should also be holding the wire in place.

7. Proceed with each shell, testing the placement of the wires before making the holes. You can do this by holding the shell in the palm of your hand with the wire wrapped over its surface.

8. When all the shells are wired in place, cover the inside of the tray with white household glue or epoxy cement. Press the backing holding the shells into position in the tray, and let dry for 24 hours. You might want to balance a book on top of the shells to add weight and pressure to the whole thing. For glueing see page 43.

9. Add two picture framing up-eye screws to the back of the tray, one on each side and 2¼ inches down from the top edge. String picture wire between them and hang from a picture hook on the wall.

10. You can make several displays. Paint the surfaces of the frames different colors, and use any color velvet as a background. Velvet is particularly good as the holes made in the fabric will not show, and the soft texture contrasts with the crisp outlines of the shells.

UNLINED SHADOW BOXES

These boxes can be bought in variety stores or craft shops. They are often of unfinished wood, allowing you complete freedom to match or contrast the color with room furnishings or wall. Before buying, check the sizes of the boxes, then look over your shell collection and decide which box is best for your needs.

You can display a collection of one type of shell—lining them up in rows or placing them in a design. You can also mix several types by planning a geometric design. Or, you can arrange several shells into a "picture," with a large sea fan on one side sheltering several shells on the bottom of the sea. A dried seahorse adds interest as it floats in the sea above the bottom area.

Tools and Materials

Practically no tools are needed—only paint brushes and plastic paint spreaders.

Materials, too, are at a minimum. A wooden box, shells, colored enamel, flat paint or stain, an epoxy resin which is sold under several names—waterproof sealant, clear varnish resin or marine resin (all clear and transparent). You will also need sandpaper, screw eyes and picture wire.

Steps

1. Clean and prepare your shells, if necessary. Then arrange them on a sheet of paper within a pencilled outline of the box.

2. Sandpaper and finish the shadow box in your choice of paint or stain, giving it two or more coats and sandpapering the surface smooth between each layer.

3. When the box is hard and dry, put it flat on your working surface with the opening facing upward. Be sure the box is absolutely level—*this is important*. If the box is not level all the clear resin will run to one side, leaving an uneven surface.

4. Pour in the clear resin to the depth of ⅛ inch. Check the drying time suggested on the label of the can. Let dry until tacky. Then working swiftly but very precisely, put each shell in its final place as you cannot move anything once it has touched the epoxy surface.

5. When the design is completed, press each piece lightly to be sure that everything is solidly attached to the resin. Let the box dry in position and do not attempt to move it until thoroughly hard—at least 24 hours, and longer in damp weather.

FIG. 16. *A Sea Fan shadow box.*

Variations

1. If you have a good collection of Cone Shells, place them in a circle in the center with the points facing inward. Make two rows if you have enough shells, putting smaller cones on the inside circle. If not, add a circular-shaped shell in the middle—a flat Snail Shell, or a bulls eye, or a sand dollar. If the center circle is not too large and you feel the corners are empty, add a Scallop Shell in each corner with the bottom at an angle facing inward toward the cones. Olive Shells, or turrets, can be substituted for cones or used to supplement the Cone Shells.

2. Sea fans or sea branches are often found on Florida beaches attached to a shell with a hard, red-coral-like substance. Embed in the epoxy with its bottom almost touching the edge of the box. You might want to dribble some sand along the bottom area. Add small shells and one or two slightly larger ones. A sea horse and a floating strand of seaweed will add to the underwater look.

SHELL DISPLAY TABLE

One of the loveliest ways to display a collection of shells is in a deep, glass-topped, felt-lined shell table—really a shadow box on legs. Since the shells do not have to be held in place, you can change your design frequently. The glass top keeps them fresh and dust-free. You can choose any shape table as long as there are sides at least four inches deep between the top and the legs.

Tools and Materials

You will need the standard woodworking tools—hammer, saw, screwdriver, rasp, pliers, paint brush, scissors and ruler.

The materials list starts off with a table and shells, then proceeds to: plywood and a sheet of heavy plate glass (both cut to fit the size of the table top), wood molding if the table does not have a top edging, sandpaper, felt, white glue and furniture glue, nails, shellac and paint.

Steps

This project will follow step-by-step the conversion of a particular table, but the directions will apply to any size or shape which has deep sides—just make your own adaptations. This table had been a mahogany-finished 20½ x 39½-inch coffee table with leather over a plywood top. The leather was stained and worn and the mahogany finish was scratched in places. There was a narrow molding around the edge of the top, and a deep side molding between top and legs.

Fig. 17. *A coffee table display of shells under glass.*

1. Make several connecting drill holes along one side of the top to make room for a small wood saw. Cut away the wood top flush with the inside edge of the molding. File the edges smooth with a wood rasp.

2. Turn the table over. Make a newspaper pattern of the bottom area, measuring flush with the outside of the side molding and allowing a cutout around the legs.

3. Put the pattern over your fresh piece of ½-inch plywood. Mark wood and cut out with the saw. You can have your local lumberyard cut the plywood to the exact rectangular size, and then all you have to do is to cut out the corners.

4. Apply furniture glue to the bottom edges of the side molding and around the matching surface of the plywood. Put plywood in place over the bottom of the table and hold firmly with thin furniture nails all around. Dry well before proceeding to the next step.

5. Refinish the outside molding, legs, and the outside surface of the bottom plywood. If you are using a color be sure that the lining felt is a compatible color—either matching or contrasting. One of the deciding factors may be the available colors of felt. A bright billiard-table green was my choice as shells look well against it. The table was enameled in a clear lemon yellow. Shellac the inside and outside surface of the plywood to prevent warping.

6. Make two measurements of the inside depth of the table, using a piece of string, so you will know how much felt you will need. Measure from the edge of the narrow top molding, down the side, across the length and up the other side. Next measure the width area the same way (Fig. 18). Buy felt.

7. Using these measurements make a newspaper pattern. Cut out a triangle at each corner so the sides will meet evenly. When you cut the felt, allow a little extra material at the corners and all around the edges. One can always cut away, but will never be able to add on.

8. Now for the cutting out. If there are any wrinkles in the material, steam them away *before* cutting. Put pattern over the felt and cut out. Fit it inside the table and trim away any excess material.

9. Remove felt and cover sides and bottom with white glue, using the edge of a piece of cardboard as a spreader.

10. Carefully put the felt back in position, smoothing and pressing down the material, working from the center out to the sides. Use the dull edge of a knife to make the joining edges and corners sharp. Press down all over with the palms of your hands so that good contact is made between glue and felt, removing all air bubbles. Let dry very well—at least 24 hours.

11. In the meantime, clean and prepare your shells, if necessary.

12. Arrange your shells against the felt.

13. Place the glass, which has been cleaned and polished on both sides, over the top. It should fit down into the top molding a bit, and so be held from slipping off in either direction.

14. Put table in position in your room and enjoy looking at your very own indoor seashore.

Variation

If you are all thumbs when it comes to tools, look for the Parsons table design that is also often called a terrarium table or a growing table. It has a sunken center covered with a sheet of glass. Line the sunken center with felt, arrange your shells, put the glass cover back on—and your shell table is complete.

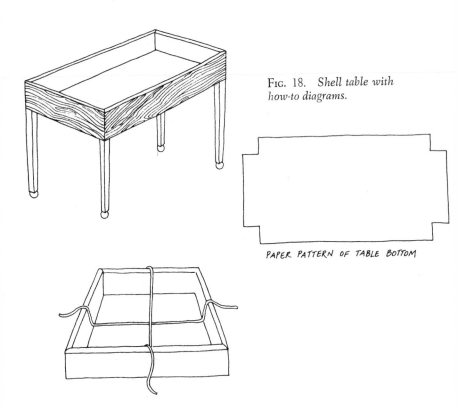

Fig. 18. *Shell table with how-to diagrams.*

PAPER PATTERN OF TABLE BOTTOM

AN ORIENTAL SHELL CABINET

A cabinet with shallow drawers is a good place to keep a shell collection organized and free from dust. Cabinets can be small or large, depending on the size of your collection. If you start with a small cabinet—just a few drawers—plan ahead so that other modular units can be added to it, as shell collections have a way of growing as you add "just one more shell."

We had a collection that was spilling out of storage boxes, piled up in stacked jeweler's trays and displayed on table tops and in a shell table. We started looking in second-hand shops for spool cabinets although the drawers would be too shallow for some of our shells. Our solution was a second-hand wooden dental cabinet. Bits of the veneer were peeling off, there was a mirror with scroll work on top, and the bottom edge was weighted with a facing of dark green marble with one section missing. But it had eighteen drawers in three rows at the top, a deep square one in the center, and two rows at the bottom with six deep drawers. They all slid in and out smoothly and their original glass knobs were intact. A treasure!

We decided to transform the cabinet, giving it an oriental look with black enamel and brass corners, and we painted the inside of the drawers in bright colors. The inside bottom of each drawer was lined with contrasting felt.

Here is, step by step, the transformation of the cabinet from a dental tool holder to a shell holder.

Steps 1 to 4 are for our particular cabinet—the rest of the directions apply to any wooden cabinet or chest with shallow drawers. If you want to change a dental cabinet into a shell cabinet, look in the Yellow Pages of the telephone book under Dental Supplies—and dental cabinets will be listed. And if you are lucky, someone might have second-hand wooden ones on sale.

Tools and Materials

You will need the standard woodworking tools—hammer, saw, screwdriver, rasp, pliers, paint brush, scissors and ruler.

The only materials were a foot-square piece of veneer, epoxy cement, plastic wood, paint, sandpaper, brass corners and felt.

Steps

1. The top mirror and shelf arrangement was removed—luckily it was only screwed onto the back of the cabinet.

2. The bottom marble facing was not a structural part of the front and sides, so it was easily removed by taking out the long screws that held the pieces in place. Plastic wood took care of the screw holes.

3. We then washed down the whole thing, inside and out, removing any loose pieces of veneer. Then we sandpapered the old mahogany varnish down to a smooth surface.

4. Next step was to cut small, matching pieces of veneer to match the irregular missing pieces. In some cases we had to make a tracing-paper pattern. They were held in place with epoxy cement, and when dry the edges were sandpapered smooth to blend in with the rest of the surface.

5. Next, we removed all drawers and gave their fronts (placed in a horizontal position) three coats of black enamel, sandpapering between the first two coats.

6. The outside of the cabinet was also painted with the three coats of black enamel and sandpapered after each of the first two coats.

7. Now came the fun part. The drawers were placed flat on the floor, and the inside of each one was painted a different bright color (there were some repeats of color). Using oil colors in tubes, we were able to vary the colors—orange, red, pink, green, turquoise blue, light blue, purple, yellow and many variations in between.

8. Once the insides of the drawers were dry, contrasting felt was fitted into the bottom and held in place with white glue.

9. Brass corners were added to the outside of the cabinet.

10. A flat brass oriental design that I had made was nailed to the center square drawer, and a brass drawer pull was substituted for the glass one.

11. Then came the happy time of arranging the shells so that each drawer became a display, the bright color of the paint and felt contrasting with the gleaming black of the cabinet. The drawers were often left open in various parts of the cabinet to show off the shells. But before you put your shells in the cabinet, clean and prepare them, if necessary.

Fig. 19. *A dental cabinet that became an oriental-style shell cabinet.*

2

Making Shell Fantasies

SHELLS used decoratively become conversation pieces. They remind us of the seashore, recreating a tropical mood of sun, malachite sea, palm trees and lush flowers. There are many clever ways to use the extra shells collected at the beach—the treasured loot of a vacation. Some designs are useful, others are for fun, and all add a new, creative dimension to the display of a shell collection—gathered or bought.

Tools and materials used in this chapter are mostly simple household ones. Since the projects are diversified, not all tools are used in every case and the materials also vary, so tools and materials will be listed as needed at the beginning of each project. But there are some processes that are used over and over in this chapter and throughout the book, and these are given below.

DRILLING HOLES IN SHELLS

One of the trickiest but most important skills to acquire is drilling a hole in a shell. Some shells can be bought all drilled, and others have been worked on by the occupants of drill shells who have drilled through them to get at the succulent meat inside. But if you haven't bought mechanically drilled shells or gathered "holey" shells on the beach, here's what you do. First, a word about drills.

Drills

Drills are made in three styles. One is hand-operated with a handle attached to a gear wheel. This is very similar to a manual egg beater. The second is an electric drill in the shape of a gun with a pistol grip and trigger release. The third and smallest is a craft type of electric drill with a separate motor, a flexible shaft, and a pencil-grip drill head. It is a simplified version of a dentist's drill.

The bit--the working end of a drill--is removable and comes in several thicknesses to make any size of hole you need. Buy separate bits for wood and for metal.

How to Drill

Experiment first with discardable, or "throwaway," Scallop or Clam Shells. Test the size of the drill-bit, the pressure to exert and the best way to brace the shell.

An electric hand drill is the fastest and easiest one to use. And a *cork tile*, ½ inch thick, makes the best working surface as it absorbs the drill's vibrations and thus minimizes the danger of shattering the shell. You'll find that most shells are a lot sturdier than they look, and can take considerable pressure.

If you are making a hole in a bivalve (a single or clam shell type), drill from the inside out as there will be less chance of cracking the shell. But if you try drilling on the convex side, the drill may slip on this outer curve, or the shell might crack as you press down against the open space below. When you are using an electric drill, brace the shell with your other hand so it will stay in position on the cork surface.

Fig. 20. *Beginning a hole in a shell with an electric hand drill.*

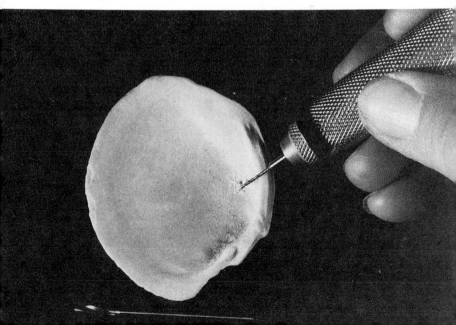

Make a mark on the shell where you want the hole to be. Start your drilling with a fine drill-bit, which will drive through the shell much faster than a thicker one. Press the bit point firmly against your mark and start the drill. At first, use a slow speed and light pressure, increasing both as you feel the quality of the shell. Once a good indentation has been made, lift up the bit, put a drop of water in the depression, place the bit in position and drill away until the hole is made all the way through. If you want a larger hole, rock the drill-bit around the edges, or replace the bit with a larger one.

Some of the Gastropods (snail-like shells) will be drilled at the bottom of the opening called the canal. Again, drill from the inside so that your drill-bit will be penetrating the area that rests solidly on the cork tile.

If you are using a hand drill, which needs both hands to operate, then you will have to clamp the shell against the cork tile. Bend thin, small *nails* into a right angle and press the points into the cork close against the edges of the shell until firm contact is made with the top of the shell by the horizontally angled end of each nail, thus holding the shell firmly in place.

SAWING SHELLS AND METAL

Two types of saws are useful for the projects in this and other chapters. A *jeweler's saw* is like a small hacksaw, but it is smaller and the blades are very fine. This is ideal for cutting metal, both sheet and rods. The blades are inserted between the wing nuts top and bottom, with the teeth facing out and down. In sawing, the blade is held upright by the handle. Pull the blade through a piece of wax to lubricate it, make a nick with a file at the edge of the metal, pull the saw downward to start the cut. The upward sweep is lightly done as this is not a cutting motion, then pull downward firmly and with a slight inward pressure against the metal. Follow this routine until the metal is cut through.

In working with a jeweler's saw, one uses a *bench pin*—a short length of wood with a keyhole opening, which is attached to a working table by a clamp.

Small, regular *wood saws* are useful in other projects and easy to use. The cutting motion is at a slanting downward angle, with the cutting action on the downthrust.

There are also small *craft saws* with a 1 x 6-inch blade, which fits into a handle.

Use a jeweler's saw for sawing shells like Clam Shells, or other thin flat varieties, but insert a slightly heavier blade in the frame.

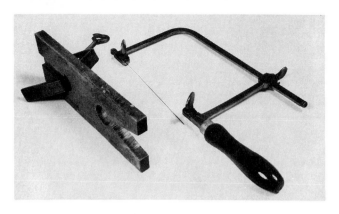

FIG. 21. *A bench pin and jeweler's saw.*

GLUEING OR CEMENTING

The most all-around useful glueing medium is *epoxy cement*. There are a number of products on the market. These are sold in two ways: one type is a single tube which only has to be applied; the other type is supplied in two tubes and only becomes effective when equal amounts from each tube are mixed together. I prefer the latter as it seems to create a stronger bond. Beware of the super-strength single tube epoxy cements with wildly extravagant claims; these must be handled very carefully, and fingers must be protected by rubber gloves as the material will glue fingers together, and only a surgeon can cut them apart! Epoxy will bind non-porous materials together permanently, and is ideal for sticking shells to glass, metal, plastic, wood, or shell to shell.

White glue is a water-soluble material that dries clear, and is sold under several trade names—Elmer, Sobo, and many others. It is useful when one is working with paper, cloth, braid or cord.

No matter which adhesive you use there are several rules to follow.

1. Read label directions carefully as they vary from product to product.
2. Mix epoxy cement on a piece of aluminum foil, mixing the two parts with a toothpick or wooden stirrer for at least a minute.
3. Apply enough glue to hold parts together, but not so much that the pieces are flooded.
4. Carefully wipe away any cement or glue that squeezes out at the edges.
5. On porous surfaces, coat well and let white glue sink in a bit, then add another layer before putting pieces together.
6. Allow plenty of drying time. Epoxy usually needs 24 hours for a good hard joining.

43

FIG. 22. *Equal parts of epoxy cement components are squeezed onto aluminum foil.*

FIG. 23. *Mixing the two parts of epoxy cement together.*

ANNEALING WIRE

See Chapter 4, page 106, for a complete description of this process.

NIGHT LIGHT

A low, softly glowing light is produced from a small electric bulb inserted in a good-size shell—a Horse Conch (*Fasciolaria gigantea*), Trumpet Triton (*Charonia variegata L.*), or two other conchs—a southern one, a Lightning Conch (*Busycon perversum*), or the northern Knobbed Pear Conch (*Busycon caricum G.*), or any other large Snail Shell 9 to 12 inches long.

Tools and Materials

No tools are needed unless the shells are in bad condition and need cleaning and scraping.

Materials, too, are very simple: a large shell as described in the first paragraph. A two-prong light plug with an off/on switch; overall length is 2¼ inches. A small rounded-point bulb, approximately 1¼ inches long. Double-ended extension cord, long enough to reach from the electric source to the night light area.

FIG. 24. *A foot-long Conch* (Fasciolaria papillosa) *from the west coast of Florida.*

Steps

1. Clean and prepare the shell, if necessary.
2. Insert the bulb in the two-prong light plug, and attach the plug to the female plug on the extension cord.
3. Slip the bulb and plug inside the shell.
4. Attach other end of extension cord to the power source.
5. Turn on switch and your lamp is a floating shell in a dark room.

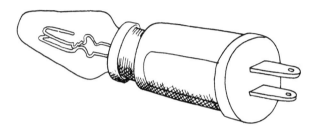

FIG. 25. *Drawing of socket and bulb and installation inside the shell.*

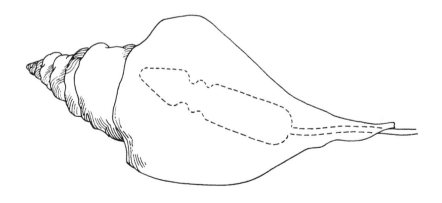

45

CLAM SHELL SOAP DISH

This is a great soap dish for a summer cottage or for a seashore-style bathroom. Mine is a fossil Clam Shell.

Tools and Materials

An awl for digging holes. A toothpick to mix epoxy cement, and a paint brush to spread epoxy resin.

For the makings: a large Clam Shell, 5 or 6 inches long, either a Surf Clam (*Spisula solidissima*), or a Quahog (*Venus mercenaria*). Three Limpet Shells (*Diodora*)—standard size. Epoxy cement and colorless varnish resin.

Steps

1. Clean and prepare the shells, if necessary.

2. The three Limpet Shells are the feet that will support the Clam Shell. Put the three shells on the working surface, open end down. They should be placed in a triangular pattern—two in front which is the long end of the Clam Shell, the third in back, toward the pointed center of the large shell. Balance the Clam Shell on top.

3. Once you have achieved the proper placement of the three shells so that the open face of the Clam Shell is level, mark the curved bottom of the large shell in the three places where the limpet points are in contact. Use a felt-tipped pen.

4. Turn over the Clam Shell and, using a drill, a small awl or other sharp, pointed tool, scoop out a small pit at each pen mark.

5. Mix epoxy cement following directions on the two tubes. Put a drop in each pit, and a drop on the end of each limpet. Press the limpet points into their pits by bearing down on the Clam Shell. Rock the Clam Shell a bit to be sure that the limpet "feet" are even, then let everything dry undisturbed for 24 hours.

6. Turn the Clam Shell over and add a ring of epoxy at the joining area of each limpet, smoothing it over ⅛ inch of the limpet as well as the Clam Shell surface. Let dry in this upside-down position for another 24 hours.

7. Turn right side up and paint inside of the Clam Shell with a *thin, thin* coat of clear, epoxy resin. (A thick coat will run down and "puddle" in the middle of the dish.) Put on three *thin* coats, letting the epoxy dry well between the layers.

8. Turn over and put one thin coat over the back of the Clam Shell, and over the limpet feet. Let everything dry very well, and your dish is then ready to hold a cake of soap.

Fig. 26. *From the Pliocene period, a fossil Clam Shell found near Lake Okeechobee in Florida.*

Fig. 27. *Finished soap dish showing Limpet Shells (Diodora) in position.*

A CORAL STRAND

Beachcombing on a tropical beach will turn up all sorts of strange and beautiful things from the sea. Creamy coral, like ridged sand dunes, sea branches of pale yellow or cerise pink and limpets like little Fiji Island huts were all found on a beach in Puerto Rico, and together form a fantasy island scene.

Tools and Materials

Toothpick to mix and apply epoxy cement.

A flat piece of coral. A piece of yellow sea branch. Three limpets (*Diodora*) of assorted sizes. All can be bought in shell shops if you are far from a beach. Epoxy cement, or plastic putty such as Plasti-Tak.

Steps

1. Clean and bleach coral.

2. Sea branches always have a base of fibrous brown material with which they are attached to rocks or coral at the bottom of the ocean. Find the right spot on the coral for your "tree." In the model it is a high spot toward which the lines of coral converge. Attach with epoxy cement for permanence. If you are making one-time table decorations, attach everything with white plastic putty, which can be easily removed.

3. Arrange the three Limpet Shells and attach them to the coral with either epoxy cement or plastic putty—and your scene is done. These scenes make amusing place setting decorations for a festive Hawaiian luau dinner.

4. If you are breaking up a large sea branch into several "trees," use the plastic putty or Plasti-Tak as a base for each tree, mounding it up and marking lines with a fingernail.

A HANGING PLANT HOLDER

This is a monumental plant holder. The Queen Conch (*Strombus gigas*) is a large, heavy shell, usually 8 to 12 inches long, found in the West Indies and Florida. We found these three in Puerto Rico. The outside is a deep yellow-tan and the inside an incredible porcelain rose pink. Since the three shells are going to be tightly sealed together with no chance of drainage, plan to keep your plant in a separate pot, which will be set into them. Hide the pot with sphagnum moss. Or you can fill the shell area with loose sphagnum moss over a layer of gravel and grow a fern directly in the hanging shell container.

Tools and Materials

A drill for making holes. Chain-nose pliers for attaching hooks to chain. Thin dowel for mixing epoxy cement. Spreader or brush for applying epoxy resin.

Materials needed include, of course, three large Queen Conch Shells, bought at a shell shop or by mail order. Strong brass chain with links about ½ inch long. Buy the chain after you have made your container, as you can then check the length needed by temporarily hanging the holder with heavy cord. Four strong hooks, either plain or S hooks. Epoxy cement. Clear pouring resin. Wire or heavy cord for holding shells together while cement is hardening. Newspaper, blocks of styrofoam or tissue paper, for bracing shells.

Steps

1. Clean and prepare the three shells, if necessary.

2. Drill a hole, ¾ inch below the edge of the wing, and close to the body of the shell. Make a hole in the same spot on each shell. See page 40.

3. Before cementing the shells together, make sure that they are dry and that no water has collected inside.

4. Put one shell flat on the working surface with the aperture facing up. Brace it with crumpled tissue paper, or newspaper.

5. The second shell will fit into the first one. Pointed ends should be together, and the cone area resting on the edge of the wing. Arrange the bracing—newspaper, blocks of styrofoam, or tissue paper—as this second shell will be partly on its side, with the aperture facing inward and only slightly up in the air.

6. Mix up a good quantity of epoxy cement.

7. Heavily smear the contact areas of the two shells with epoxy cement, and place them together again. The weight of the second shell should be enough to maintain good contact. Let dry undisturbed for 24 hours. Remove bracing material.

8. Repeat with third shell. This one is placed flat on the working surface. Apply epoxy heavily to the wing edge of the second shell and the third shell, and place them in position, under and over the bottom shell.

9. At this point you will want to hold the shells together with light wire or cord wrapped around the outside. Let them stay unmoved for the 24-hour drying time.

10. Shells are now held together, but you will want a thick coat of epoxy resin filling in the empty areas between the cone of one shell and

the wing of another. Balance the three shells so that an area between two shells forms a trough. Fill with transparent colorless pouring resin in successive thin layers, allowing time for each layer to dry before adding another.

11. Repeat this process with the other two troughs.

12. When everything is hard and dry, pour resin in the area where the points of the three shells come together.

13. When dry, test with a cord to check the length of chain needed, and then buy the brass chain. Attach hooks through the drilled holes. Cut chain and attach it to the three hooks, bringing the three pieces of chain together on the fourth hook for hanging. Add plant, and hang container in a window area.

SURREALISTIC SEASCAPE

This decoration developed from a scuba-diving-plus-beachcombing expedition on Martinique, but all the materials are available at shell shops or by mail order. It is a very effective decoration that does not demand special shells—and strangely-damaged shells add to the total effect. The only *must* is a Sea Fan (*Gorgonacea*).

Tools and Materials

Wire cutter and chain-nose pliers. Hammer and nail or a hand drill, whichever is available for making holes in the wood base. Toothpicks for mixing epoxy cement.

A lavender or cerise-red sea fan, not more than 10 inches high. Several types, sizes and colors of shells. You may not use all of them, but have enough so you can pick and choose for your design. A piece of driftwood, which can be a piece of tree or a chunk of waterworn lumber from a wrecked boat. The one shown in the picture is a weathered, split piece of 3 x 5 x 15-inch wood. Twelve-inch length of brass wire. Epoxy cement, baby oil, clear nail polish (optional for covering shells) and sandpaper.

Steps

1. Check your driftwood for any rough spots or splinters, and sandpaper these areas. Wash off to remove any salt scum or tar.

2. Clean and prepare shells, if necessary, and oil them very lightly, unless you decide to give them a high shine with clear nail polish.

3. Move shells around on the driftwood until you have a pleasing design. Suggested combinations include: orange, black and calico scal-

lops; Moon Shells of several sizes and types; bubbles; astartes; coral; winged pearl oysters; mussels; mangelias; egg-shell cockle; limpets; small dog whelks. The fan should be placed upright, to the left or right of center. With epoxy cement, glue some of the shells to short lengths of brass wire so that they will be above the surface of the wood, acting as a counterbalance to the fan. (See Fig. 30.) If you have double shells use them here, so that the seascape is two-sided.

4. Once your design is decided upon, attach the shells to the wood with epoxy cement and let dry for 24 hours. If you are adding shells to the sides of the wood, put these on first, turning the wood so that the side becomes the horizontal face. Let dry for 24 hours before turning back to the final position of the wood.

5. To attach the brass wires holding shells, make holes in the wood using a nail or a drill. The nail or drill-bit should be smaller than the supporting wire, as the wire will then be forced into the hole for a firm and steady fit.

6. The last piece to add is the sea fan. Mix enough epoxy to make a puddle for the natural fiber base of the fan. Let it thicken a bit, then transfer to the wood so it forms a deepish puddle. You may even want to gouge out the wood a bit so that the epoxy is contained. Put the base of the fan into the liquid, scooping up some of the epoxy around the edge and over the side of the base. Hold it in place with two angled books braced against each other with the fan in between. Brace the bottom of the books with other books so they won't slip. Let everything dry for 24 hours. Add a second coat of epoxy around the base of the fan, spreading it over onto the wood. Check the other shells and add epoxy if necessary. Again let everything dry for 24 hours, and your seascape is complete.

7. An additional optional step is to cover all the shells with a thin coat of clear nail polish as a finishing touch. (If you want this high shine, do not oil the shells.)

BARNACLE FLOWERS AND PLANT HOLDER

Clusters of barnacles are often washed ashore on southern beaches. These are much larger than the northern variety found on dock pilings and rocks below high-tide level. The cluster shown here is 3½ inches across and 4¼ inches high, and is creamy white with dull red petal-like surface designs.

The barnacles can be tinted to look like crocus flowers and set into a small flower pot that has been filled with plaster of Paris, with moss pressed into the top surface.

FIG. 28. *Coral, Limpet Shells and a sea branch form a coral strand* (*page 48*).

FIG. 29. *The finished plant holder, showing the three Queen Conch Shells* (Strombus gigas) *in position* (*page 48*).

FIG. 30. *A surrealistic seascape of shells, sea fan and driftwood* (*page 50*).

FIG. 31. *Bracing the sea fan in position while it dries.*

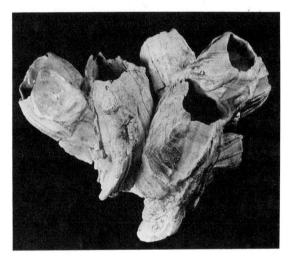

FIG. 32. *A large, white barnacle cluster.*

FIG. 33. *Barnacle flowers (left) and a barnacle plant holder on a piece of driftwood (page 54).*

Also, the clusters are big enough to serve as holders for very small plants such as cactus, or succulents of the hens-and-chickens variety, or *Sinningia pusillas,* or shamrocks for St. Patrick's Day. Fasten the barnacles to a piece of driftwood to hold them upright.

Tools and Materials

Soft water-color brushes for adding color. Tablespoon and bowl for mixing plaster of Paris. Toothpicks for mixing epoxy cement.

One or more barnacle clusters. Transparent waterproof ink in flower colors—yellow and purple. Plastic flower pot, round or square, or a decorative china container. Sheet moss, plaster of Paris, small limestone or marble chips. Epoxy cement, aluminum foil. Plants, soil and driftwood. Clear nail polish.

Barnacle Flowers: Steps

1. Make sure the barnacle cluster is clean and the surface free from lime deposits.

2. If you are going to stain the barnacles, wait until they are dry. Apply ink, either full strength or diluted with water. Hold cluster upside down and stroke on color with a soft, round, water-color brush. To approximate crocus flowers, stain some of the barnacles yellow and others purple. Let dry.

3. Mix plaster of Paris and pour into a white plastic flower pot or decorative china container. If there are holes in the bottom of the pot, cover them with clear plastic wrap before pouring in the plaster. Fill the pot to within ¼ to ⅜ inches from the top. To mix, see page 211.

4. When the plaster is almost hard—that is, soft enough to press the barnacles into the top but not so soft that they will sink too far down—add the barnacles in the center. Make sure they are deep enough to be held steady. You may have to support them with angled books. Press small lime chips or sheet moss over the surface to cover the plaster, but be sure the plaster is firm enough to support the chips, or they will sink under the surface.

5. Let everything dry until surface is no longer damp and cool.

Plant Holder: Steps

1. Fasten the barnacle cluster to a small piece of driftwood. Try to have as many barnacles as possible facing upright. First dig out a hole in the driftwood, using a wood gouge, a knife or whatever comes to hand. Hold the cluster in place with epoxy cement, bracing it until dry—about 24 hours.

2. If you want a shiny surface, coat the outside of the barnacles with clear nail polish. Two separate coats are best with drying time in between. Let final coat dry for 24 hours before adding plants.

3. Buy very small cactus or succulents. Put a little packaged cactus soil in the bottom of each barnacle. Add the plant, then fill cup to within ⅛ inch of the top. Cover the remaining area with dry gravel. Do not water. Wait a week until the plants have recovered, spraying them lightly with water once a day. At the end of the week add very little water with an eyedropper. Water once a week, barely moistening the soil. Remember, these are desert plants and will rot if they receive too much water. If plants show any signs of shriveling, increase the amount of water. Put in bright sunlight. Look around the plant shops for other very small plants that would fit your cluster. See the list of suggestions at the beginning of this project.

SUPER-EASY GLASS TILE MIRRORS

To make the simplest of all mirrors, use glass tiles. These are available at household stores, discount or department stores. They are often sold with a peel-off paper backing that exposes the sticky surface which can be attached to the wall. Leave the paper on as you will want mobility for your mirror. You can add stick-on hooks to the backing. The shells are placed directly on the tile in a border design.

Tools and Materials

Tools are very simple. You will need soft brushes, compass, pencil, ruler and scissors.

Shells—either an assortment of types for the design shown in the photograph, or Mussel Shells as shown in the drawing. Mirror tile—12 x 12 inches or 10 x 10 inches. Stick-on picture hooks and picture wire. Epoxy cement, white glue and clear epoxy resin. Aluminum or gold paint. Ammonia or rubbing alcohol for cleaning glass. Clear nail polish, stencil paper, double-sided sticky tape and masking tape.

A Mussel Mirror: Steps

1. For a 10-inch square tile you will need approximately 20 Mussel Shell halves of assorted sizes. For a 12-inch tile, 28 shells will be enough. At least four should be about 3¼ inches long, and the others ranging in size down to 2 inches. Gather shells at the beach or a bay area. If you live inland, go down to your local fish market and buy one or two dozen

mussels. Make *moules à la marinière* for dinner and save the shells. Choose the mussels carefully so you'll have the right assortment of sizes. The shells can be used for other projects, too.

2. Clean and prepare shells, if necessary.

3. Make a paper pattern the size of your tile mirror. For a 10-inch size, cut out a center circle 6¾ inches in diameter, and for a 12-inch tile, an 8-inch circle.

4. Place your shells on the paper pattern in their final arrangement, the pointed ends facing inward to an imaginary dot in the center. The four largest shells are placed one in each corner.

5. The shells can be left in their natural blue-black color, then covered with a coat of clear nail polish. Or, you may decide on aluminum or gold paint.

6. The mirror must be free of all grease and finger marks. Wipe with either clear, plain ammonia or with rubbing alcohol.

7. There are two ways of attaching the shells to the clear, mirrored surface. For both of them you will need to prepare a circle of oiled stencil paper—6¾ inches in diameter for the 10 x 10-inch mirror; 8 inches in diameter for a 12 x 12-inch mirror.

METHOD ONE: Put the circle of oiled paper in the centered position on your tile, holding it in place on the underside with small pieces of double-sided sticky tape.

Mix epoxy cement. Pick up the large shell for the upper left-hand corner. With a toothpick, lightly run epoxy over the edge of the shell and put it in position on the tile, rocking it in place so that a full impression of the edge is left on the mirror. Lift up. Now add a narrow ribbon of epoxy on the mirror, following the line left by the shell edge. This ribbon should be high enough to flow up the edge of the shell, creating a solid bond. Re-epoxy the shell edge, running some epoxy up over the edge on the inside and outside of the shell. Place shell in position, settling it into the ribbon of epoxy. Repeat the process with the other three large corner shells.

Now fill in with the small shells, again attaching them as you did the four large shells. You may find it better to mix the epoxy in small quantities, enough to do two or three shells at a time.

When you have finished, let the mirror and shells stay *undisturbed* for 24 hours. If you have a large enough flat book, you could put it *very carefully* over the whole mirror tile, to rest on top of the shells, adding a steady downward pressure while they dry.

METHOD TWO: This involves flowing on a layer of clear epoxy resin in the shell area, with the mirror center protected with a strip of oiled

FIG. 34. *The all-sorts tile mirror (page 58).*

FIG. 35. *Mussel mirror designs.*

OILED PAPER

ADD CLEAR EPOXY RESIN

Oiled paper on mirror.

Diagrams of an easel back (Step 9, page 58).

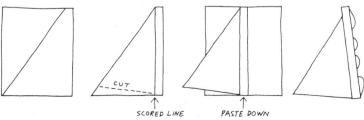

CUT

SCORED LINE

PASTE DOWN

stencil paper held firmly in position on the inside of the circle with tape. Paint a thin coat of the resin over the uncovered mirror surface outside the circle. When it becomes tacky, press shells firmly into the surface and let them dry undisturbed for 24 hours.

8. For both mirrors add the stick-on hooks to the back upper edge, just below and in from the corners. Attach the hooks upside down, so their points are facing downward. String picture wire between the hooks and hang on a wall hook.

9. If you want the mirror to rest upright on a table, cut a right-angle triangle 9 inches high and 4¼ inches at base out of a piece of cardboard. Score lightly with a razor knife ¾ inch in from the edge, along the 9-inch height. Now, cut off a thin triangle from the bottom edge, from the scored line to the outside angled line, going from nothing to ½ inch on the slanting line. Check the angle of the standing mirror by holding this easel back against it temporarily. If too upright, cut off more cardboard at the bottom, making a sharper angle to the bottom line.

Cover the ¾ inch area with white glue or epoxy cement. Press against mirror back, so that the scored line is in the middle of the paper covering the back of the tile, and the wide bottom is touching the bottom of the tile. Let dry, in a flat position. When dry, reinforce the edge with masking tape.

To keep the easel support in position, paste a piece of ribbon to the center of the support on the pasted-down side. Straighten the easel into position, and paste down the other end of the ribbon to the tile back. This will have to be in two operations as the first pasted-down end will have to dry. Hold the second pasted-down end in position with a piece of masking or sticky tape.

All-Sorts Tile Mirror: Steps

The directions for this 12-inch square mirror are the same as for the Mussel Mirror, except that you'll use an assortment of shells, ranging in color from warm ivory to yellow to orange. See Fig. 34 for a suggested placement of shells.

A TOUR DE FORCE MIRROR

A shell-decorated mirror frame can be a fun accent in a room that is light and airy modern, or if tucked in amongst pictures, it adds a Victorian touch like a froth of sea foam. There are as many possible designs as there are shapes and sizes of mirrors and varieties of shells.

This design is based on a curved-top rectangular mirror with a plain wood frame, 3 inches wide, with a narrow inner molding bordering the mirror. Two entirely different ways of constructing the basic frame shape will be described, and from these methods you can develop your own mirror shape, depending on the materials you have available.

Tools and Materials

You will need the standard woodworking tools—saw, hammer, screwdriver, pliers, plus paint brushes and narrow metal or rubber spatula. Wooden stirrers and toothpicks.

A mirror, no smaller than 6¾ x 10¾ inches. A plain, flat wooden frame. Narrow molding or half-round dowel—measure the three straight sides on the inside of your mirror frame. Balsa wood or ¼ plywood.

One 5-inch white Scallop Shell, and six 3-inch white Scallop Shells. These are sold in department or specialty stores as canapé or Coquille St. Jacques baking shells. They are imported from Japan and are pure paper white. You will also need about 80 white, glossy Lined Tellin Shells 1¼ inches long. These can be a combination of tellins and *Dosinia elegans*, or little white Lucine Shells. (Any beach-gathered shells should be cleaned and prepared.)

General supplies include: sandpaper, shellac, flat white paint, gesso powder, epoxy cement, picture hooks and wire.

Fig. 36.   *White Coquille St. Jacques Scallop Shells.*

Fig. 37. *Pure white shell mirror frame (two versions) and a diagram of the frame.*

Steps

1. The curved top mirror frame can be achieved by several means.

   a. A picture framing shop can make it to your specifications.

   b. You can buy a flat-surfaced picture frame of the approximate size—one that is not made of molding at several levels. Try to find one slightly smaller in its outside edge measurements, and add a thin layer of balsa or plywood to support your final design.

   c. Or, you can buy plywood and make your own—cutting it out yourself, or having the local woodworking shop cut the curved top piece to your specifications. Add the curved top mirror, edged with molding, in the center of the board.

   d. Or, you may find an old frame complete with mirror in a second-hand shop. Adjust the shell design to fit the measurements.

2. If the frame has been made for you, check the finish to see if it is smooth. If not, sandpaper it, wipe off the wood dust, and cover the raw wood, front and back, with a coat of shellac. Let dry, and sandpaper again. Now cover with two coats of flat white paint, letting the paint dry between coats and sandpapering the first coat before adding the second. Make sure the white is a good flat white surface—if it tends to have "gray" areas, add another coat. Repeat on the back of the frame. If only one side is painted, the wood will warp. Paint molding around mirror. Add mirror and molding to top surface of flat wood frame.

3. You are now ready to add the shell decorations. First, sandpaper the top surface of the flat white paint so it is slightly roughened. This will enable the epoxy cement to form a firmer bond.

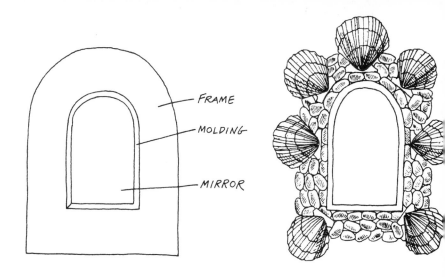

FRAME

MOLDING

MIRROR

4. Make a tracing-paper pattern to the exact dimensions of the finished frame—from the outside edge to the edge of the inner molding.

5. Arrange the Scallop Shells on the pattern in their final position. The 5-inch shell is at the center top with its upper edge stretching slightly above the frame area. The 3-inch shells are placed around the frame. The two top shells are placed at the upper corners over an imaginary angle line which would run through the center of each shell. The two bottom shells are also placed over an angled line, but off center, so that only about one-third of each shell is on the side part of the frame and two-thirds on the bottom area. The other two shells are placed on the sides, halfway between the top and bottom shells. Outline the shells on your pattern with pencil lines.

6. Lay the paper pattern over the frame and mark the areas of the Scallop Shells with small dots, strategically placed. Use a sheet of paper, one side of which has been blackened with lead pencil (in place of carbon paper) to transfer these dots to the wood.

7. Cut ½-inch square pieces of balsa wood to the exact depth of the center of each Scallop Shell. Cement into position on the frame as attachment supports for the shells. Try out under the shells before finally adding the epoxy cement.

8. Epoxy the large shells in position and let dry for 24 hours.

9. Fill in the intervening spaces with white Tellin, Dosina, or Lucine Shells—all one kind or a combination. Most of the painted background should be covered with a pleasing pattern of white shells.

10. Let everything dry. Add hooks on the back and hang your elegant mirror in a favorite place where you can admire it.

FIG. 38. *A pair of white Tellins, a Murex and two Cone Shells.*

A PEAR IN A PARTRIDGE TREE

This is a coffee table decoration, a half-round tree made of outspread double shells—white tellins or small thin clams or Dosinia Shells. They look like birds with their wings outstretched. The pear is a single, small yellow Cone (*Conus*) or orange Murex Shell hanging from the edge of the tree. The trunk is a gold-painted wooden dowel set into a white plastic flower pot filled with plaster of Paris.

Tools and Materials

Small saw, sharp razor-blade knife, mixing bowl, tablespoon, toothpicks and a small water-color brush are all the tools you will need.

The materials needed are equally simple. Approximately 20 to 25 double Tellin Shells or other flat or very slightly curved white shells—not more than 1½ inches wide. One ¾-inch long yellow Cone or Murex Shell. (All beach-gathered shells should be cleaned and prepared.) One styrofoam ball 4 to 4½ inches in diameter. Small white plastic flower pot 3½ inches high. A 9- to 10-inch long wood dowel, ⅜ to ½-inch in diameter. Odds and ends needed are plaster of Paris, epoxy cement, gold paint, fine wire and sticky tape or masking tape.

Steps

1. With a sharp knife or small saw cut the styrofoam ball ⅜ inches below the halfway mark. First mark the cutting line with a felt-tipped pen so your cut will be even. Discard the smaller part.

2. Outline a ⅜- or ½-inch circle—depending on the diameter of the dowel—in the center of the flat surface of the styrofoam. Cut out a core 1 inch deep. Insert the wood dowel temporarily in the hole.

3. Hold the "trunk" of the tree upright in the flower pot to check its visible length—that is, between the top of the flower pot and the bottom of the half-round of styrofoam. Cut off any excess dowel.

4. Remove the wood dowel trunk from the styrofoam, and cover the surface with gold paint. Let dry well. Add a second coat if necessary.

5. Mix enough plaster of Paris and water to fill the flower pot. If there are holes in the bottom of the pot, cover the inside bottom area with a piece of plastic wrap. To mix, see page 211.

6. Pour the plaster into the pot, filling to within ⅜ inch of the top. Hold it steady until the mixture solidifies enough to support the dowel. Let plaster dry until it is hard and no longer feels cold and damp to the fingers.

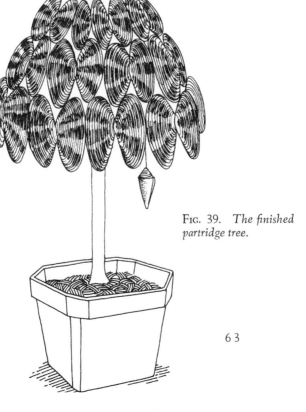

Fig. 39. *The finished partridge tree.*

63

7. Paint the inside of the center hole in the styrofoam with epoxy cement. Also coat the top 1-inch section of the dowel. Carefully put the half-round of styrofoam onto the dowel, making sure it is level all around. Wipe off any excess epoxy that may start to run down. Let epoxy harden for 24 hours.

8. If you are lucky enough to have all double shells, you will find that they are joined together at the top points—this becomes the center of the two shells when they are flattened out. Spread the shells and put a drop of epoxy at this joining to strengthen it. Do this also with the double shells that are not joined by this membrane. Spread the shells out on a grid of nails, so that the epoxied points will be suspended in space.

9. If you do not have double shells, match up the singles by size to approximate double shells. Epoxy the points and dry as in Step 8.

10. The first row of shells will be at the bottom edge of the half-round of styrofoam. The joining points should be just at the bottom edge of the foam. Make a mock-up of the first row, using small pieces of sticky or masking tape at each shell side to hold the pairs temporarily in place. You may have to adjust the spacing a bit to fit in a complete row of double shells.

11. When the final pair is in place, make shallow cuts in the styro-foam at each shell side, so the shells can be pressed into the foam a bit.

12. Mix epoxy cement. Remove tape from only one pair of shells at a time. Using a toothpick, place epoxy in the cuts and around the edges of the shells, then press the shell edges into the cuts in the styrofoam. Replace tape to hold the shells while they dry. Repeat process with each pair of shells. Let row harden overnight. Remove tape when shells are dry.

13. When you place the shells in the second row, the joining point should be just at the "wing" top of a double shell in the first row. This means that the V between the double shells will be filled with the left and right halves of two double pairs. You may even want to slightly overlap the shells of the second row onto those of the first row. (See Fig. 39.) Repeat the mock-up, cutting, fitting, taping and epoxy routine as in Steps 10 to 12.

14. Continue the rows of shells until the styrofoam is covered.

15. Attach a thin piece of wire or thread with epoxy to the opening in the Cone or Murex Shell. Let dry. Stick wire or thread into the bottom edge of the styrofoam and hold in place with a drop of epoxy cement. The top of the cone should be ⅜ inch below the lowest edge of the shells.

FLUTTERING BUTTERFLIES

Pastel-colored Coquina Shells (*Donax variabilis*) are used in this design. They are found along the shore from North Carolina south to Florida and across the Gulf to Texas. They seem to wash in with a wave, then burrow rapidly into the sand. The empty double shells are found on the beach in all shades of yellow, pale lavender, blue, green, red brown and rose, some with sun-ray effects. Put them on the ends of fine wires to form clusters of colorful butterflies.

Tools and Materials

Chain-nose pliers, small wire cutters, hack or small hand saw, hand drill or hammer and fine nail, paint brushes and toothpicks.

Materials start with up to a dozen double Coquina Shells of assorted colors. Approximately 6 feet of fine brass wire, bought by the spool in hardware or craft shops. A small block of balsa or pine wood, or a block of cork conglomerate. A 3- x 4¼-inch cake of white soap. Shellac, and enamel paint. Sandpaper, and crocus cloth. Epoxy cement. Tracing paper.

Steps

1. Clean and prepare shells, if necessary.
2. Make a rough pencil layout of the placement of the shells. Remember that there can be some overlapping as the wires will be different lengths.
3. From this layout you can determine the size of your block. The block shown here is 3½ x 5 inches and 3 inches deep.
4. First, you will need to shellac the wood block, then paint or stain it, sandpapering between each coat. The color choice is up to you. The cork block will be left in its natural brown color, unless a stark dull white surface is what you yearn for.
5. Cut the wire into twelve pieces of various lengths—from 7 inches to 3¾ inches—remembering that at least ¾ of an inch will be thrust into the block, and about 1½ inches will be used to form two loops to attach to the shells. The wire should be strong enough to hold the shells, but fine enough so as not to overpower them.
6. The next step is to make the end supports for the shells. At the 1½-inch mark, bend the wire at right angles, using the chain-nose pliers. Then, on this horizontal piece, ¼ inch in from the vertical wire, make a second bend downward and around, ending up with the end of the wire in a horizontal position going the other way after crossing over the verti-

cal wire. Bend this end at the ¼-inch mark, up and around so that the end of the wire is returned to the vertical wire—and you now have two loops on each side of the vertical upright. These loops form the supports for the double shells.

7. Repeat the bending process with all the wires.

8. Curve the loops a bit, using pliers and your fingers, so that the wires fit snugly into the inside curve of each shell.

9. Keep some of the loops in a level horizontal position and tip others a bit upright or to one side, so the "butterflies" will float at different angles.

10. Make a final mock-up using a cake or two of soap (depending on the size of your base support) to determine where the wires will go. You may find that you have completely changed the placement of the wires, departing from your first tracing-paper plan.

11. Mix the epoxy cement on a piece of aluminum foil and let it thicken a bit. Smear a little of the epoxy on the top of each loop, and also on the matching area inside the shells. Press shells firmly in place and stick wire ends into the cake of soap at the best angle to maintain the shells in a horizontal drying position. When dry, add a second layer of epoxy over the wire loops and onto the shell area. Let dry for 24 hours with the shells in a horizontal position.

12. Now that the shells are attached to the wires, rearrange the wires on the soap in their final position. Cut a piece of tracing paper the exact size of your base to make the working pattern. Gradually cover the soap with the paper, starting at the narrower left edge. Lift up each wire, put the paper in place, and plunge the wire through the paper and back into its original hole. Once the pattern is complete, reverse the process to remove the paper. Lay paper over final base, and mark through the holes with pencil or felt-tipped pen or with a white pencil for the cork block.

13. Make holes ¾-inch deep in the wood or cork with the hand drill or a fine nail hammered in. The hole should not be larger than the wire.

14. Transfer wires to proper holes, being sure to remove any soap from the wires. Now is the time to make any adjustments—to shorten wires or switch butterflies.

15. Go over the wires with the crocus cloth, giving them a final polish.

16. Lift up each wire in turn, put a drop or two of epoxy cement in its hole and replace wire. Let everything dry for 24 hours.

Fig. 40. *Colorful Coquina Shell* (Donax variabilis).

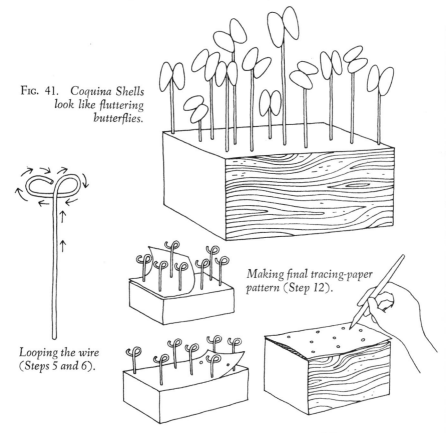

Fig. 41. *Coquina Shells look like fluttering butterflies.*

Looping the wire (Steps 5 and 6).

Making final tracing-paper pattern (Step 12).

SHELL MOBILE

You can let your imagination go on this project, combining shells you have gathered or bought. Buy packets of white Japanese Scallop Shells or the pressed, translucent Philippine shells known as Capiz or Kappa. Combine them with Fig Shells (*Ficus papyratia*), white Olive Shells (*Oliva*), or Angel Wings (*Barnea costata*), plus Limpets (*Diodora*). Disk Shells (*Dosinia*) which are found along the Eastern seaboard can look interesting too. Hang the shells from metal crosspieces and let them swing and twirl in the summer breezes.

Tools and Materials

Simple, simple tools—you'll need only a wire cutter, pliers, hand drill, scissors and toothpicks.

Shells of your choice. Sturdy wire—cleaner's hangers are very good. Black thread or nylon fishing line or brightly colored wool or cord. Epoxy cement.

Steps

1. Clean and prepare beach-gathered shells.
2. Mobile frames take many shapes and sizes. The simplest is two horizontally crossed wires, held together with a wrapping of fine wire reinforced with epoxy cement. Shells are hung from these wires with varying lengths of thread or cord. This process is a balancing act, so that the metal arms do not tip one way or another. A hooked length of wire or heavy cord forms the hanger for the mobile.
3. You can add other wires, off center, balancing them with heavier shells. Take a look at some of Alexander Calder's mobiles to spark your imagination.
4. Add one or two hanging strings of Limpet Shells, held in place by knots through the top holes of the shells.
5. White Olive Shells can be spaced along clear fishing line. Hold them in place with epoxy cement.
6. If your mobile is in an air passageway, add narrow rectangles of glass to the ends of 3 or 4 strings of shells, and there will be a soft tinkling sound as the wind blows.
7. The shells can be finished with either a thin rubbing of baby oil or with clear nail polish.

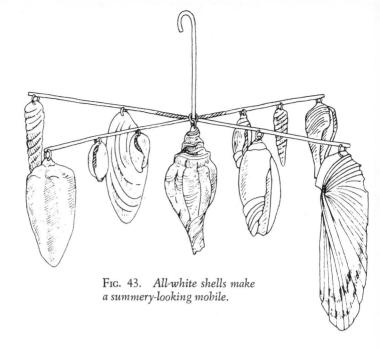

FIG. 43. *All-white shells make a summery-looking mobile.*

FIG. 42. *From top to bottom: an Angel Wing* (Barnea costata), *Olive Shell* (Olivia), *two views of a Fig Shell* (Ficus papyratia), *and a white Scallop* (Pecten).

69

Fig. 44. *Fine lines decorate this shiny white Southern Dosinia (Dosinia concentrica).*

A BEACHCOMBER'S RECYCLING PROJECT

Shells decorate the side of a straw basket salvaged from a gallon bottle of Spanish wine. It makes a great holder for potato chips, popcorn, fruit, chunks of French or garlic bread. Also, the basket becomes an unusual cover for a plant pot.

Tools and Materials

All you need is a razor blade knife, a drill, large needle and toothpicks.

Approximately 16 large, flat shells 2½ to 3 inches across of the dosinia or lucine type, or round clam varieties (*Venus*) will cover the basket. Wine bottle straw covering 8½ to 9 inches in diameter. Thread or nylon fishing line, epoxy cement.

Steps

1. Remove the straw basket covering from the glass wine jug. First cut away the shoulder covering down to the woven braided edge. Slip off the bottom basket. Some baskets have handles attached to the heavy top edge; keep these on as decorations.

2. If shells are beach-gathered, clean and prepare them.

3. If you have a drill, make a hole in the point of each shell. (Page 40.)

4. If you do not have a drill, turn the inside of the shell upward on a flat surface. Attach a length of thread, cord or nylon fishing line to the inside of the shell—from the top to bottom—with epoxy cement, leaving 6 inches at each end. Let dry for 24 hours.

5. Tie shells to the basket in two spaced-out rows, placed so they're not lined up one above the other. Bring the thread through the basket and tie on the inside. You may need a large-eye needle for this. For the drilled shells, run the thread through the hole and through the basket, and tie on the inside.

6. This simple design is very effective with its almost round white shells against the tan wicker work of the basket.

7. You can add an additional decoration around the top edge with a row of limpets.

Fig. 45. *The finished basket hung with shells, ready to hold a tropical plant.*

SOUTH SEA ISLAND HAT AND BEACH BAG

Add a band of small Cowrie (*Cypraea*), Bubble (*Bulla occidentalis*), or Limpet Shells (*Acmaea*) to a straw hat. Make a sunburst in the middle of a bag with a combination of brown-and-white Land Snail Shells, yellow Cone Shells (*Conus*) and tan Olive Shells (*Oliva*). This is an elegant design set against an orange straw bag or on a circle of orange felt in the center of a natural straw bag. The sunburst shells can match the hat band using a combination of cowries and bubbles.

Tools and Materials

Tools are down to a minimum—scissors, toothpicks and a needle.

To make the designs you will need small tan Cowrie Shells ¾ to ⅞ inches long, Bubble Shells or Limpets, all approximately the same size— up to an inch long. Yellow and white Cone Shells, and gray Netted Olive Shells (*Oliva reticularis*), approximately 1⅞ inches long. A brown-and-white flat Land Snail Shell 1½ inches wide. Satin ribbon ½ inch wide (any color you like), plus grosgrain ribbon, 1 to 1¼ inches wide, in a matching or contrasting color. Both ribbons should be long enough to go around the hat as a band. The satin ribbon is longer than the grosgrain, as it has to tuck into the apertures on the shells. A 6- or 7-inch square or circle of bright-colored felt. Epoxy cement, thread, white glue, rubber cement or plastic putty.

FIG. 46.   *An assortment of shells which can be used in this project. Clockwise, starting at the top: St. Lucian Cone* (Conus), *Netted Olive Shell* (Olivia reticularis), *Atlantic Gray Cowrie* (Cypraea cinerea), *Limpet* (Diodora), *Tree Snail from Puerto Rico, Striated Bubble* (Bulla striata).

Hat Band: Steps

1. Loop a piece of string around the crown of your hat where it joins the brim, and cut at the joining. Place the length on your working surface as a measurement for the number of shells needed.

2. Clean and prepare shells, if necessary. Place the shells over the string, side by side, until the string is covered.

3. You will need a longer length of ½-inch satin ribbon, as a loop of ribbon will be tucked into the aperture of each Cowrie Shell and held with epoxy cement. The exact amount is hard to estimate, but start with a piece at least twice the length of the string and then add a little extra for good measure.

4. Mix epoxy cement.

5. Pick up the first shell. Smear epoxy on the bottom and inside of the aperture. Place the ribbon over the edge of the shell, 1 inch from the end. With the flat end of a clean toothpick tuck a fold of ribbon into the aperture, making sure it comes in contact with the wet epoxy cement. Place a drop of epoxy between the folds of ribbon to hold the two sides together. Repeat with the next shell, being careful not to pull on the glued end of the ribbon (or you will pull it out of the first shell).

6. The Cowrie Shells will roll, so put a large drop of rubber cement under each one as you put it in position on your working surface. This will hold it steady as the epoxy dries, and can be rubbed off afterwards. Or use pieces of plastic putty.

7. When all the shells have been attached to the ribbon, let it stay undisturbed for 24 hours.

8. Put a thin coat of white glue along the bottom of the satin ribbon and press it down the center length of the grosgrain ribbon. Let dry overnight. If you rush these two drying processes, the shells may pop off later on.

9. Attach ribbon to the hat by tacking with thread. Turn under ends and hold with thread. You may want to add a line of white glue to the back closing.

Beach Bag: Steps

1. Cut a 7-inch circle of bright-colored felt.

2. Mark the center of the circle. Cover back of Snail Shell with epoxy cement and press onto the felt in the exact center of the circle.

3. Surround the Snail Shell with alternating Cone and Olive Shells—six of each in a sunburst pattern. Hold them in position with epoxy cement, aperture side down. Let dry undisturbed for 24 hours.

Then check the adhesion and add more epoxy around the edges of the shells, if necessary.

4. Attach felt to the straw bag by covering the entire back of the circle with white glue, and pasting it down on the straw. After the glue has dried, tack down the felt with thread.

Variation

The shells can be applied directly to the straw bag with epoxy cement.

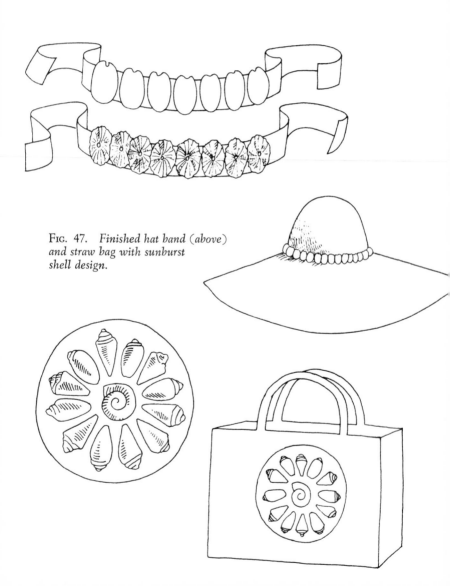

FIG. 47. *Finished hat band (above) and straw bag with sunburst shell design.*

Fig. 48. *Two Lucine Shells* (Codakia) *form a modern sculpture.*

BLACK-AND-WHITE SCULPTURE

Two stark white shells, a block of black painted wood, plus brass wire form an understated, modern sculpture.

Tools and Materials

Drill, hammer, wire cutter, soft paint brushes and a teaspoon.

Two pairs of Lucine (*Codakia orbicularis*) or Dosina Shells, in two sizes. Two lengths of 15- or 16-gauge brass wire, 6 and 8 inches long. A 4 x 5-inch rectangle of wood, 5 inches high. Shellac, dull black paint, liquid clear pouring resin, sandpaper, crocus cloth, a thin nail, epoxy cement, felt-tipped pen, white grease pencil and clear nail polish.

Steps

1. Make sure the shells are clean and prepared. They should be sparkling white.

2. Shellac the wood block. Let it dry, then sandpaper away any roughness.

3. Paint the surface with black paint. Let the first coat dry, then sandpaper until smooth. Cover with a second coat of paint and let dry. Sandpaper and add another coat if surface is not an even black.

4. Use sticky tape to hold one shell of each pair in position on the

7 5

ends of the wires. Move shells up and down the wires until you have the right relationship of shell to height of wire—but remember that 1 inch of the wire will disappear into the wood block. Mark the wire with a felt-tipped pen or metal scriber just at the bottom edge of the shell.

5. Remove shells from wire. Put a half of each pair, hollow side up, on your newspaper-covered working surface. Spoon clear pouring resin into each of these halves, filling it half full. Let dry. Then add more resin, bringing it to the level of the edge. When the resin is tacky, place each wire in position in the center line of the shell, balancing each free end on a piece of wood, pencil, or whatever is the right height to keep it level. Let the halves with their wires dry until the resin is hard.

6. Fill the other halves of the shells with clear pouring resin in the same way. When the second pouring is tacky, take the already hardened halves with their embedded wire, turn them upside down and join to their other halves in their final position. Support the free ends of the wire as you did earlier. Dry for 24 hours or longer, if necessary.

7. When you are sure the pouring resin is good and dry, lift up the shells and check to see that the wires are solidly held in the resin. If not, or if the edges of the shells are not solidly held together, add epoxy cement where needed. Let dry.

8. Move wire and shells over the top of the wooden block until you find the right place for both shells. Mark block with white grease pencil. Drill holes in the block, or hammer in a fine nail to make the holes for the wires. The holes must be a little smaller than the wire.

9. Polish both wires with crocus cloth. Wipe clean and cover with clear nail polish to prevent tarnishing. Let dry.

10. Put a little epoxy cement in each hole of the wood block. Slip the wires into place, turning the shells to the angle you want. Let dry—and your modern sculpture is finished.

Variation

Make a cardboard box and cover it with black Contac paper. Fill with pebbles for weight and proceed as above with the wooden box.

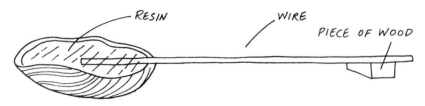

Fig. 49. *Detail of supporting center wire while resin in shell is drying.*

Fig. 50. *A baby Horseshoe Crab 2 inches wide,
a dried whelk egg case and a starfish.*

SEASHORE CHRISTMAS TREE

Go beachcombing in spring, summer and fall for the dried materials
for your special, evocative table Christmas tree.

Tools and Materials

Small water-color brush, scissors or wire cutter and toothpicks.

All sorts of shells, Crab Shells, starfish, seaweed, whelk egg cases and
small Horseshoe Crab Shells (*Limulus polyphemus*). Gold paint (sold
in small bottles in art, crafts, stationery or variety stores). Thin wire or
fine gold cord or nylon fishing line. Epoxy cement, and white glue.

Steps

1. When you are on a beach, look along the high-tide line for flotsam
areas, and pick up dried Crab Shells, long strands of seaweed, especially
the type with air bladders. Sometimes you'll find starfish, and in the early
spring on some beaches there are small 2½-inch Horseshoe Crab Shells.
You can even find lengths of nylon fishing line from lost tackle. Whelk
egg cases are long strands made up of round sections strung together like

Hawaiian leis. Mussel Shells, Scallop Shells—particularly the gray or white types—and small Clam Shells can be found on northern beaches along the Atlantic coast. If you are far away from beaches, shell shops have some or all of these dried materials.

2. Wash beach-gathered materials in fresh water to remove salt and sand. Let dry well. Store the well-dried material in a covered box until needed.

3. When you are ready to decorate a small table tree, get out your treasures. Check the joints of the crabs—if any are loose, hold them in place with a drop of white glue.

4. Cover each piece of dried material with gold paint. Use a soft water-color brush to apply the gilt. Let dry well and then apply a second coat if necessary. Let dry a second time.

5. Attach nylon fishing line, gold cord or thin wire to the gold ornaments with epoxy cement or white glue. You might want to glue two horseshoe crabs together along their edges, to make a rounded ornament. Matching Mussel or Scallop Shells can be handled the same way.

6. Hang the ornaments on the tree—starfish at the top. Gilded seaweed is hung as garlands. The whelk egg cases make a wreath for the base of the tree. Place the other shells on the ends of the green branches.

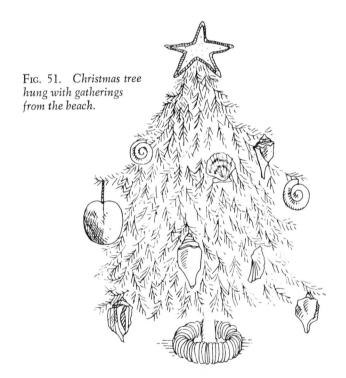

FIG. 51. *Christmas tree hung with gatherings from the beach.*

FIG. 52. *The surface of this large Cowrie* (Mauritia Mauritiana calxequina) *is hard and brilliant, with a mottled design in brown and tan.*

A COWRIE BIRD

The body of this amusing bird is a porcelain-shiny spotted Cowrie Shell (*Mauritia mauritiana calxequina*) from the Pacific Ocean. It is held in a cradle of wire that swoops up to become the neck and head, while twisted brass wire forms the legs and feet. This is not super hard to make, and the result is very elegant, a boutique type of decoration. To guide you through to a triumphant conclusion, the step-by-step description has to be detailed—so take heart and try this design.

FIG. 53. *The dark brown underside of the Cowrie Shell.*

Tools and Materials

Two chain-nose pliers, small wire cutter, rubber mallet or ballpeen hammer, small metal file, wooden spoon or wooden-handled kitchen tool, metal scriber and a felt-tipped pen.

A 3-inch-long Cowrie Shell with a broad brown edge and mottled brown-and-ivory top. A 3½-inch-high wooden spool of brass wire—15- or 16-gauge is a good thickness. You will also need between 3 and 4 feet of 22-gauge straight wire for cross-bracing. Crocus cloth for polishing the wire, masking or sticky tape, tracing paper, epoxy cement and clear nail polish.

Steps

1. Look closely at your Cowrie Shell. It has a larger opening at one end, and this will be the back of your bird. Many cowries are humped off center. That is, from the larger opening the shell slopes up to an off-center height, and then drops off more or less abruptly to the other opening, for all the world like a camel's hump. This drop-off area is the front of your bird's body.

2. Cut five pieces of wire, each 15 inches long, and four pieces, each 18½ inches long.

3. Anneal the wire. (Page 106.)

4. Take out any kinks in the spool wire by squeezing and straightening with your fingers, or gently tapping with a rubber mallet or the ballpeen hammer whose working surface has been covered with a piece of felt or heavy leather to protect the wire from gouges. If you have bought straight lengths of wire, ignore this step.

5. Now make a pattern on which the wire body cradle will be formed. About 5 inches above the bottom margin of a 20-inch-long piece of tracing paper, trace the outline of your shell. Turn the shell over, paper over the bottom, and fill in the outline of the center opening. Remove shell, and trace over your two outer lines so that you have a complete pattern on the "wrong" or "under" side of the paper.

6. On the right side of the outline, draw a line on your pattern 1¼ inches from the back of the shell. On the left side make a line 1½ inches from the back point.

7. Now start the formation of the cradle to hold the shell. (This also includes the legs, neck and head.) Measure off 2 inches at one end of each wire, and make a mark with a black felt-tipped pen, a scriber or a small piece of tape. This is the wire that will form the bird's tail, protruding from the back of the shell.

8. Bend a short wire to follow the curve of the center aperture of the shell, allowing it to extend 2 inches beyond the pattern of the shell. The wire at the other end will become part of the neck and head. Hold *both ends* down on the paper with tape. You may find it easier to tape the whole sheet of paper down against your working surface.

9. You are going to have three rows of wire on each "bottom" side of the center wire. (The other two wires will be on the sides of the shell.) The first long wire on the right follows the inside curve about $\frac{5}{16}$ inch in from the opening. Let the 2-inch length stay outside the shell outline and hold down with the tape.

10. When you get to the 1½-inch mark, hold the wire in place with tape. Now, clamping the wire tightly with the pliers, bring up the free end at right angles to the paper. Measure off 1¾ inches, then curve the wire downward again until it touches the paper. Straighten it out with another right angle turn so it can proceed up the curve of the shell bottom pattern. This loop will form part of one of the bird's legs. Hold end of wire down with tape.

11. Repeat this process with the next long wire on the right—tape down, loop wire for leg, curve along shell bottom and then tape down the free end of the wire.

12. Finally curve the third short wire just inside the outer edge. No loop. Tape at both ends. And one side is finished.

13. Repeat this process on the left side of the shell pattern. But the two loops will be made at the 1½-inch mark.

14. Without distorting the lengthwise position of the two middle right-hand wires, bring the loops on the right side together. Hold them firmly together with the pliers at paper level. With the other pliers, loosely twist the two loops together. Later on you may want to tighten the twist, as you decide how long the legs should be.

15. Repeat this process on the left side. Now on to the shell.

16. The final two wires will hug the sides of the shell, approximately ¼ inch above the edge, and these will be formed *on the shell itself.*

17. Starting with the 2-inch mark on the wire resting at the back opening of the shell, tape the wire onto the shell at this point. Press the wire against the shell following the contours, and hold the wire in position against the side with pieces of tape. Bring it up a bit higher in the front as the two wires will form the back of the neck.

18. Repeat with the other side.

19. Temporarily remove wires from the shell and set aside.

20. The next step will hold the cradle wires together. Measure width

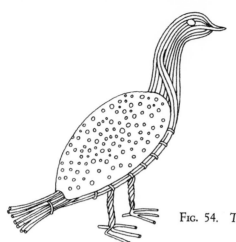

FIG. 54. The finished cowrie bird.

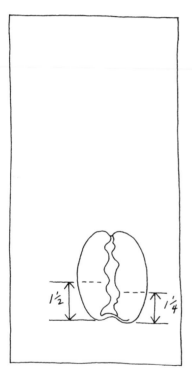

Tracing shell, underside
(Step 5).

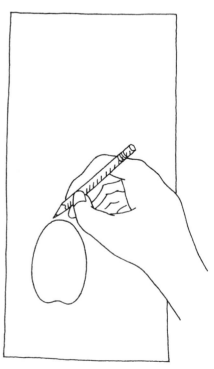

Tracing shell, right side
(Step 5).

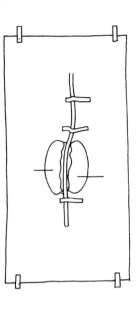

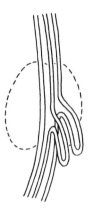

Forming the cradle of wires on the paper pattern, and a close-up of the leg wires (Steps 7 to 13).

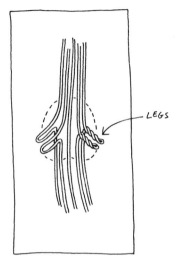

LEGS

Twisting leg wires (Step 14).

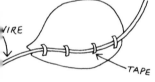

WIRE

TAPE

Placing wire on outer edge of shell (Steps 16 and 17).

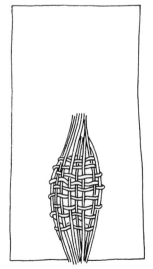

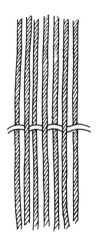

Weaving the cradle wires together, and a close-up of one strand of weaving wire in place (Steps 20 and 21).

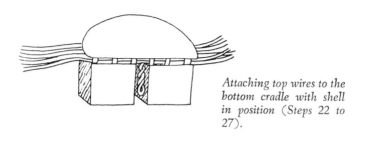

Attaching top wires to the bottom cradle with shell in position (Steps 22 to 27).

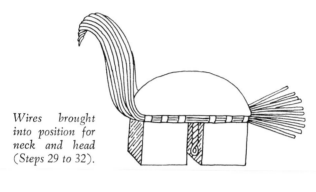

Wires brought into position for neck and head (Steps 29 to 32).

Detail of leg and foot (Steps 34 to 36).

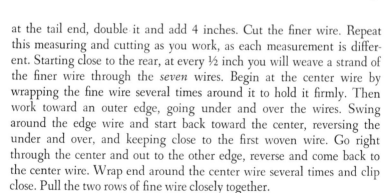

at the tail end, double it and add 4 inches. Cut the finer wire. Repeat this measuring and cutting as you work, as each measurement is different. Starting close to the rear, at every ½ inch you will weave a strand of the finer wire through the *seven* wires. Begin at the center wire by wrapping the fine wire several times around it to hold it firmly. Then work toward an outer edge, going under and over the wires. Swing around the edge wire and start back toward the center, reversing the under and over, and keeping close to the first woven wire. Go right through the center and out to the other edge, reverse and come back to the center wire. Wrap end around the center wire several times and clip close. Pull the two rows of fine wire closely together.

21. Repeat this step every ½ inch, until you reach the front of the shell pattern.

22. The next step is to attach the two side wires. Turn the wire cradle over. The best working platform for this process is a flat one, with a crack in the middle to hold the wire legs—two bricks, two blocks of wood, two small folding tables pushed together, two loaf pans turned upside down,

two recipe boxes or file boxes—look around and see what you can devise.

23. Cut a 5-inch length of the fine wire and bend in half. Twist the wire by holding the top end near the loop with a pair of pliers, while you twist the two wires together from the other end using your other pliers.

24. Now comes the process that will make you want another set of hands. You'll feel all thumbs, but it can be done. Put the shell in position on the cradle. At the 2-inch mark, tape one of the side wires to the cradle tail wires. At this point slip the first twisted wire under the top cradle wire, bring it toward you, wrap it once around, ending up with the length of wire on the outside. Hold the side wire firmly with a thumb or finger so it will not be pulled out of place, and wrap the twisted wire once around, then down inside next to the shell, over the cradle wire, once around, and then under the shell. Fasten off and clip any excess wire, but wire end should be hidden under the shell. Now hold this area in place against the shell, using tape.

25. If this wire has been the right length, cut nine more 5-inch lengths.

26. Proceed forward to the neck, repeating the process with four of the wires. You'll have to judge the placement of the last wire as it all depends on where the neck starts.

27. Turn the shell around to the other side, and again starting at the tail area, attach the other five twisted wires.

28. You now have your shell held securely in the cradle, with the 2-inch tail wires at one end and the wires that will form the neck and head at the other end of the shell. So far, so good!

29. At the front of the shell, pull the two side wires into an upright position practically at right angles to the shell. They will form the back of the bird's neck.

30. Hold the round handle of a wooden spoon or small screwdriver parallel to the two wires, and curve the other seven wires upright to form a hollow wire cage, which is the neck of the bird.

31. To make the head, curve the front wires forward in a right angle at about the 2½-inch point and follow with the other wires curving out and forward. Bring all the wires tightly together to make a beak. You will have to file the ends of the wires to bring them closely together. Tape the wires just behind the point—approximately ⅜ inch. Squeeze wires tightly with a pair of pliers and add epoxy cement to them at the end. Let dry and add more epoxy, building up a clear, triangular epoxy beak.

32. Wrap a piece of thin wire around one of the heavy wires to form an eye, and repeat on the other side. Or add a tiny Zebra Nerite Shell (*Puperita pupa*) on each side.

33. Now for the tail. Weave a strand of fine wire through the tail

wires at the end of the shell to bring the wires firmly together. Spread the wires out in a shallow fan. Clip the wires so the sides are shortest and the center wire the longest, then file the ends into smooth rounds. Leave the wires straight out or curl the ends with the chain-nose pliers.

34. The final part of the anatomy is the feet. Be sure the openings of the leg loops at the bottom are facing front to back. Cut two 7½-inch lengths of the heavier wire. Wrap one end of a length once around the bottom loop of one leg, bringing the wire backward from under the loop. Make a ½-inch loop horizontally backward and then forward to the leg, and make one turn around the leg loop. This is the back-supporting claw. Now make three tight ⅜-inch loops toward the front, spreading them out fan fashion. Anchor each loop with a single turn around the bottom leg loop.

35. Cut off any excess wire and file ends smooth. With the pliers held in a horizontal position, squeeze the turnings flat. File the bottom of the wires to flatten them a bit.

36. Repeat with the other leg.

37. The final step is to carefully balance your bird by angling the cradle downward at the back, leveling and bracing the legs and curving the neck to form a counterbalance. The tail may become a back-brace if you want the body at a higher-in-front position. In any case, all bending should be *steady, slow and deliberate,* to give the metal a chance to adjust to the new position, otherwise you could snap a wire.

38. Go over all the wires with crocus cloth to polish them, and take out any nicks with the file. Protect the shell with strips of typewriter paper inserted under the wires.

39. Move the two supports you used earlier (Step 22) far enough apart to allow the legs and feet to hang freely, without touching either the blocks or the working surface. Add two or three drops of epoxy cement to the joining area of feet and the legs. Let dry for 24 hours.

40. Carefully cover all the metal wires with clear nail polish. Protect shell with typewriter paper, moving the strips of paper around so that the nail polish does not form a bond. If any liquid drops on the shell, wipe off with polish remover. Let dry overnight to be sure the liquid is hard. This step will prevent the metal from tarnishing.

41. And you are done. Place it where you can admire your fantastic bird.

Variation

A humpy piece of Puerto Rican coral. Use silver-colored wire with the coral. Using either a cowrie or coral, one can make a turtle or a crab.

Fig. 55. *Spiny and smooth Cockle Shells* (Trachycardium) *from Sanibel Island in Florida.*

A COCKLE BASKET

Cockle Shells are a bit like Scallop Shells, except that they are more rounded and their ribs are narrower. In some varieties tiny spines catch and break up the light. Their colors are lush tones of ivory, beige and light tan. Piled in a wicker basket, they look for all the world like freshly gathered brown eggs. This decoration fits into a country home or a French provincial atmosphere as well as a modern one—in the dining room, all-purpose kitchen, or as a coffee table conversation piece.

Tools and Materials

Simple tools—small razor knife, toothpicks and paint brush—are all that are needed.

You will need 20 or 21 half Cockle Shells 2¾ inches long and 2½ inches wide. The number of shells will depend on the size of shells. A good assortment is: Common Cockle (*Trachycardium muricatum*), yellowish white in color with brown specks and about 3 inches long; Great Heart Cockle (*Dinocardium robustum*), yellowish brown in color with dark brown spots, from 3 to 6 inches long, so use only the smallest ones;

China Cockle (*Trachycardium egmontianum*), a beige to light yellow in color and 2 to 2½ inches long (the ribs have small scales like spines).

Also buy an oval wicker basket 7 x 9 x 2½ inches and a piece of styrofoam, either a half-round piece that fits into the basket when cut to the oval shape and mounds 6 to 7 inches high above the rim, or a 9- or 10-inch ball. Two pyramid-shaped lead fishing weights, light-tan waterproof ink, sandpaper, masking tape, epoxy cement and clear pouring or casting resin.

Steps

1. Look for a sugarloaf shape of styrofoam of approximately the right diameter or a 9- or 10-inch diameter ball. This can be trimmed to the oval shape with a razor knife or a small craft saw. Trim the bottom to a flat surface to fit against the bottom of the basket.

2. To weight the basket, cut two pyramid shapes into the bottom of the styrofoam and insert the lead fishing weights.

3. Stain the whole surface with a thin solution of light-tan waterproof ink to match the general cockle color.

4. Cover the inside bottom of the basket with epoxy cement and place the styrofoam in position. Let dry for 24 hours.

5. Place a row of shells around the edge of the basket with the curved bottom edge of the shells just inside the rim and with sides touching each other. Hold them with masking tape.

6. Make a fine cut in the styrofoam where a shell's edge is in contact. Remove the shell, fill the cut with epoxy cement and add a line of epoxy around the edge of the shell, then press into the cut. Hold in position with tape. Repeat process with each shell and then let this first row dry overnight.

7. Follow the same procedure for the next row—except that the point or beak of the shell should face downward, fitting between two points of the shells in the first row. After applying epoxy, let the second row dry overnight.

8. The third row is the last, and the curved edge of the shell now faces downward, straddling each half of two shell edges. Bring the points together in the center. After cutting line into styrofoam, apply epoxy.

9. Cover the points with one shell laid over the center top; apply epoxy and let everything dry overnight.

10. Check to make sure that all the shells are solidly fastened down. Make any repairs that are necessary. At this time you may need to add a second coat of stain if the background seems too light a color to match the shells.

11. When the ink is dry, cover the shells and styrofoam with a very thin coat of clear pouring or casting resin or clear nail polish. The liquid should just cover the shells without running.

Variation

Shells of three sizes can be used: largest on the first row, smaller next and the smallest on top. Or mix the cockle varieties—smooth and rough.

Fig. 56.   *Cockle Shells piled high in a straw basket.*

3

Decorative Boxes
You Can Make

SHELL BOXES range in design from simple wooden ones decorated with shells to jewel-like metal ones with a Fan Shell or Lion's Paw Shell cover to small ones made from double spiny oysters hinged at the back. Boxes like these are sold in boutiques and are elegant additions to the home or gifts for treasured friends.

Then there are the old-fashioned boxes out of the Gay Nineties which are still made in the Scilly Islands. All summer long the ladies gather small, brightly-colored Snail and Bivalve Shells on the beach. In the winter they fashion the decorative containers which are nothing more than wooden cigar boxes covered with shells closely fitted into a thin layer of fish glue in a sort of helter-skelter pattern so that no wood is in sight. They are great fun with an over-all orangey-tannish effect, the result of the final coat of shellac or varnish—a pure Victorian watering-place souvenir reminiscent of all the old British movies and music hall songs.

Materials, tools, directions and processes will be individually listed and described for each project, as each of the designs in this chapter has a different approach.

Let's start with an approximation of the Scilly Island box.

Fig. 57. *Assorted shells for a Scilly Island box—some from the original box mentioned in the text.*

SCILLY ISLAND BOX

A current adaptation of this charming, late nineteenth-century style.

Tools and Materials

Flat-edged paint brushes and round soft water-color brushes plus toothpicks are the simple tools needed.

Ideally, one should have a wooden cigar box with its wonderful spicy fragrance. Unfortunately, most boxes are now made of cardboard or plain wood covered with a wood-patterned paper, but craft shops sell unfinished boxes with lift-off or hinged lids, roughly measuring 5 x 8½ inches. A recycled box you can use is one that held dried Locoum Figs— a long, narrow one 3½ x 10 x 1½ inches. You can cover the raised oval center design of lettering and camels or surround it with shells, which I would do, as the contrast between camel and shells is delightful.

Lots and lots of small shells—about two cups. They should be mostly patterned or plain snail species, plus some small Limpets (*Acmaea*), Fan or Zigzag Scallops (the lower valve of both *Pecten raveneli* and *Pecten ziczac*), and Wenteltraps (*Epitonium*) for center decorations. Also add Ear Shells (*Sinum maculatum* or *perspectivum*), Star (*Astraea*), Natica species, and Clam Shells. They can be beach-worn as the final coat of shellac or varnish will hide a multitude of sins and make all the shells look glowing and colorful.

White glue or clear epoxy resin and shellac or varnish.

Steps

1. Be sure that all the shells are clean, but do not oil them.

2. Paint the inside of the box and cover with shellac or varnish, depending on which you plan to use to cover the shells when the box is finished. Use the round water-color brush.

3. Plan the center decoration for the box cover. For a square sunburst center, use four small Fan Shells set opposite each other, a round Natica or Star-Shell in the middle and wentletraps filling in the spaces between the fans. If you want an oblong design, use a limpet as your center—as it's an oval shell, it will force your design into this shape. Lay out the shells on a sheet of paper in the exact form of the final design.

4. Measure the area of this design and cover the center of your box cover with a thick layer of white glue or clear epoxy resin. Let it begin to get sticky. If some of the glue sinks into the box, add more glue as it should be deep enough to cover the outside edges of the shells to create a solid bind.

5. Once the glue is sticky, add the shells starting with the center shell, then the Fan Shells, then the wentletraps, keeping them close so the wood is covered.

6. Let the design dry completely, so that you won't disturb it in working on the rest of the box. Hardening time depends on the thickness of the glue and on the weather.,

7. Now paint on a 2-inch strip of glue along the left or right edge of the cover. Again let the glue get sticky, adding some extra if necessary. Then stick on the shells every-which-way, just so the apertures of the snails are downward, and the outsides of bivalves are upward—unless the inside is red or yellow, in which case turn the colorful side up. As you approach the inside edge of glue, let the shells form a ragged, zigzag margin to avoid a straight line which you would not want in your final cover design.

8. Add another 2 inches of glue on the other edge, let thicken and add more shells. Repeat this process until the whole box top is covered.

9. Let the top dry very well—24 hours or more—as you will have to turn it on edge if there are sides to be covered with shells.

10. While the top is drying (if it is a lift-off top), start covering the sides of the box with shells. You may want a center design on each side,

or you may cover the whole area with the random pattern—the choice is up to you.

11. Turn the box on its side so that your working surface is horizontal. Follow the glueing directions for the top of the box. You will have to let each side dry very well before moving on to the next, otherwise you'll have shells popping all over the place.

12. When working on the last two sides, place the finished side on a layer of cotton to protect the shells and to support the box so it doesn't wobble on its uneven surface. Then finish the sides of the cover in the same way.

13. Once all the sides of the cover and box are complete and dry, check all the shells to be sure they are well fastened. If any are loose or rock slightly when touched, add extra glue around the edges.

14. Now that the top is firm and dry, cover it with a very thin coat of shellac or varnish. Do not allow it to puddle between the shells. You will find that a round water-color brush is best for this purpose. (When finished, clean the brush well with paint remover, as you will be using it again and will want it to stay soft.) Let the top dry until hard.

15. Next shellac or varnish the shells on the sides of the cover and of the box, working on one side at a time, and letting it dry before moving on. You can speed things up by doing a side of the box and the cover at the same time.

16. When all is hard and dry, line the box with velvet or satin, or paint the inside with a colored enamel. And your reminder of the Victorian world is complete.

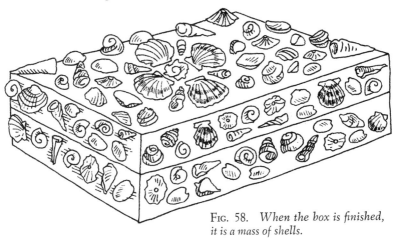

FIG. 58. *When the box is finished, it is a mass of shells.*

FIG. 59. *Florida shells on top of a small box.*

A PIECE OF THE BEACH

A recessed box cover seems to hold a section of a beach—sand and shells held permanently in place. When you look at it you can almost smell the sea air and hear the sound of waves.

Tools and Materials

Paint brush, bowl and spoon for mixing plaster of Paris, razor blade or X-acto knife, scissors, ruler and a paring knife are the tools.

An unfinished wooden box 3¾ x 4⅜ and 1¾ inches high. Wood stain plus shellac or furniture wax. Or, paint in your choice of color. A piece of white Formica or Contac paper, sandpaper, plaster of Paris, two tablespoons or so of sand, and an assortment of shells, the largest being 1½ inches long, but many of them much smaller. (Beach-gathered shells should be cleaned.) Clear nail polish, strips of balsa or bass wood, ¼ inch wide (if your box is not a recessed one).

Steps

1. If you cannot find a box with a recessed top, add a ¼-inch square wooden molding all around the outside edge of the cover. Thin strips of balsa or bass wood are ideal. Use epoxy cement to hold the molding in place, and place a weight on the top during the drying process.

2. Sandpaper the wooden box until the surface is smooth. Stain the wood a medium brown—pecan color—or paint with enamel in the color of your choice. Do not stain or enamel the recessed top. Also finish the inside to match.

3. Cover stain with shellac or varnish, or rub in furniture wax.

4. The next step is to cover the inside of the cover and the bottom of the box with the white Formica or Contac paper. Cut, and paste it in position.

5. Make a paper pattern the same size as the cover's recessed area. Place shells on the pattern in their exact position so they can be transferred quickly to the plaster of Paris once it has started to thicken.

6. Mix up enough plaster of Paris to fill the recessed area. Add a little of the stain or some tan poster paint to give the plaster a sandy color. (To mix, see page 211.)

7. Spoon the plaster into the recess, being careful not to drop any on the wooden box. If you do, wipe off the splatters immediately with a wet cloth. Mound the plaster slightly in the center. Let it settle and thicken a bit.

8. Quickly add the shells, slightly burying some in the plaster. With the flat edge of a toothpick or small knife, push the plaster up around the edges of the shells so that they will not shake loose. Again using the toothpick or knife, create an uneven surface to give the appearance of a sandy beach.

9. The plaster can be left this way or, if you do have a supply of beach sand, sprinkle a tablespoon or two over the wet plaster. When the plaster is dry, brush off the excess sand with a clean 1-inch paint brush.

10. Carefully cover each shell with clear nail polish to bring out the colors.

Fig. 60. *Coffee Bean Trivia* (Trivia pediculus) *are pink with brown spots.*

GOOD-LUCK BRIDGE DESIGN

Small Cowries or Coffee Bean Shells are formed into the classic Chinese bridge design, which fools the evil spirits into stepping off into the water.

Tools and Materials

Paint brushes, ruler, pencil and toothpicks.

Unfinished or finished wooden box. Stain, enamel, shellac or varnish. Small Cowrie Shells (*Cypraea*), or violet brown or pink Coffee Bean Shells (*Trivia pediculus* or *Quadrupunctata*) ⅜ to ½ inches long—the number depending on the size of the shells and the size of the box cover—you may need up to 48 shells or more. Epoxy cement, sandpaper and dressmaker's chalk.

Steps

1. Follow the directions for staining or enameling an unfinished wooden box as given in "A Piece of the Beach " (Steps 2 and 3), page 95.

2. Clean and prepare the shells, if necessary.

3. On a sheet of paper make a pattern the exact size of the box cover.

Draw five lines down the middle of the length of the top. The spaces between the lines will be the average length of your shells—⅜ or ½ inch.

4. Place the shells in a double row pattern. This will depend on the size of the shells and the length of the box. But as a "for instance" pattern: two rows of four shells each; then two rows of six shells each on the lower level, as the top line of this group is level with the bottom line of the first set; now back up to two rows of four shells; then two rows of six shells; and finally two rows of four shells. This design should stretch right across the length of the box. (See Fig. 61.)

Fig. 61. *Two finished box designs.*

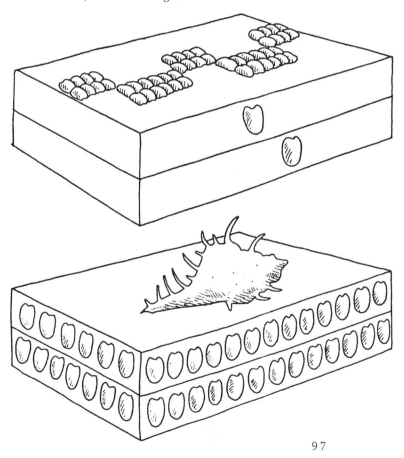

5. Once you have worked out your pattern, you are ready to transfer the shells to their permanent position on the box top. This is tricky, and your measurements have to be exact as the beauty of this design is its effect of interrupted straight lines.

6. Do not draw lines across the surface of the box cover as they will show in the areas without shells. Rather, very carefully measure the areas of your shells, and with a pin point lightly mark the top and bottom guide lines of each section of shells. Or draw the lines with a piece of dressmaker's chalk which can be washed off later.

7. Mix and paint on epoxy cement in one area at a time, keeping within the guide lines. Put epoxy lightly on the flat part of the cowries, too, and press them into the box top, keeping the two rows in exact line, using a ruler edge as a guide.

8. Repeat this process with each section of shells.

9. Let the box dry undisturbed for 24 hours.

10. Fill in around the shells with extra epoxy, so that they are held securely to the box. Again let dry for 24 hours.

11. If the top is hinged, add two larger cowries to the front of the top and the bottom side to act as knobs, putting them on each side of an imaginary center line.

Variation

Line up two rows of shells around the sides of the box. If the cover comes down halfway, place one row of shells above the split and one below. You will have to work on only one side at a time, turning each side up to a horizontal position and letting the epoxy cement dry for 24 hours before turning up the next side. While working on the last two sides place the finished side on a layer of cotton to protect the shells and to support the box, so that it will not wobble on its uneven surface. Epoxy one Murex Shell in the center of the top cover.

FAN-SHAPED SHELL BOX

This is an absolutely stunning design for a special box, combining decorative brass gallery wire for the sides, a hinged tan Mediterranean Scallop Shell for the top and a removable velvet-covered bottom. A perfect container for precious earrings or rings.

Tools and Materials

Pliers, wire cutter, scissors or metal shears, and an optional tool is a jeweler's saw.

A flat, brown Scallop Shell, approximately 4 x 5 inches long. The shell shown in the photo is quite flat, and is a warm tan-brown with lovely ribs and markings. (It was bought in a shell shop.) It should be of a generous size. You will need at least 12 inches of brass gallery wire—one or both edges should be straight—but choose the pierced design that pleases you. The width does not matter as long as it is at least ⅞ inches wide. You will also need 12 inches of stiff twine, about ⅛ inch thick. Very fine brass or gold-colored wire. A piece of stiff but pliable plastic or thin leather for the hinge. The top of a can, approximately 3¾ inches

Fig. 62. *Large brown Mediterranean Scallop Shell.*

across—a coffee can or a solid vegetable shortening can in the one-pound size. Actually, this tin circle (can top) should be in proportion to the size of the shell—and you will be buying your length of gallery wire on this basis. A piece of velvet or satin, matching sewing thread, epoxy cement and white glue. Absorbent cotton is optional.

Steps

1. Clean and prepare your shell, if necessary.

2. This step is the crucial measuring one! The tin circle for the bottom of your box cannot be larger than your shell; it should be a bit smaller so that the shell lid will overhang the sides of the box. So this step is finding the right size.

3. Next step is to cover the tin circle with fabric. Cut a circle of material ½ inch wider than the tin. Notch the fabric all around for a better fit. If you want a puffy surface, add a layer of absorbent cotton against the right side of the metal, tacking it in place with a few drops of epoxy cement. And in this case, your circle of material will have to be a bit larger to allow for the extra thickness of cotton.

4. Smear on epoxy cement in a ½-inch band all around the *bottom* edge of the metal. Place the fabric, wrong side *up,* on your working surface. Carefully center the tin circle on the fabric, epoxied side up. Bring the edges of the fabric up and onto the epoxy, working opposite sides alternately to keep the fabric even. Let epoxy dry.

5. Cut another circle of fabric with an allowance for a hem. Turn the hem under and baste it in place. Add a thin line of epoxy or white glue around the glued-down fabric. Place the hemmed circle over this side—right side of the fabric up, and put a weight over the cloth. Let dry for 24 hours—and the bottom of your box is complete.

6. Measure the outside circumference of the covered bottom and cut the gallery wire to this length, allowing ¼ inch at each end for overlap.

7. Bend the gallery wire around a can, slightly smaller than the final size. Slip off, and overlap the ends—this will take some of the tension out of the circle and make it easier to "lace" the ends together with thin wire.

8. Hold the overlapping ends together and thread the thin wire in and out of the pattern until you have a firm joining. Cover the joint and wire, inside and out, with a thin layer of epoxy cement. Let dry very well and add a second coat if necessary.

9. With epoxy cement, attach a length of ⅛-inch stiff twine to the lower inside edge of the gallery wire. Hold in place with paper clips. Let dry for 24 hours. This will be the shelf on which the bottom of the box

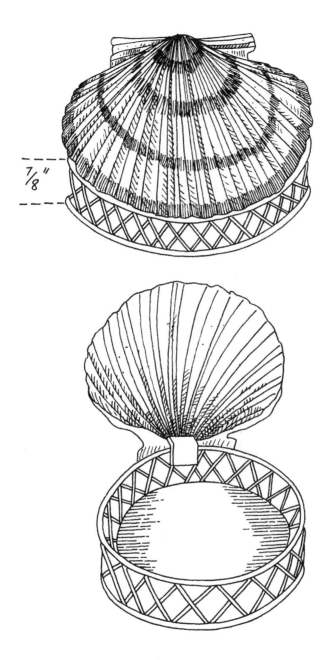

FIG. 63. Gallery wire and Scallop Shell combined in a box.

7/8"

will rest. Add a second coat of epoxy all over the twine and up onto the wire, and again let everything dry until firm and hard.

10. The final process is to attach the shell to the gallery wire using the leather or heavy plastic as a hinge. Center the flat, hinge areas of the shell at the center back where the gallery wire is joined with fine wire lacing. Depending on the width of the shell hinge area and the curve of the sides of the box, cut a piece of leather or plastic 1-inch square.

11. The shell hinge area should protrude over the side about ¼ inch, as should the rest of the shell. Cover one-half of the wrong side of the leather or plastic with epoxy cement. Let it thicken a bit. If any is absorbed, add a little more. Put into position on the inside top edge of the metal gallery wire over the back joining area. Hold firmly with a large paper clip or two until dry.

12. Now place the shell on top, then move it to an upright or "open" position. Press the upper half of the hinge material against the shell and mark the outline with chalk. Put shell flat on the working surface, the "inside" facing you. Place the gallery wire on its side, braced so it will not roll. Cover the upper half of the leather hinge with epoxy cement, and press it into position following the chalk mark on the shell. Put a weight on the leather hinge and let dry well.

13. Slip the bottom into the box, and you are finished.

Variations

You can use a Lion's-Paw Scallop (*Pecten nodosus*), or one of the flat white Scallop Shells sold in gourmet accessory shops. Also, a flat piece of brain coral can serve as a cover. In this case, as the coral is thick, you will not need to make a hinge. The coral will be a lift-off cover.

TISSUE BOX

A plastic tissue box makes a great basic shape for shell designs, and here are a number of variations.

Materials

Outside of the basic box, shells, epoxy glue and clear nail polish; the other materials are mentioned as the variations are described.

Steps

1. The plastic tissue box does not need any special preparation—just choose the color you want for your room.

FIG. 64. *Tissue box with shell design.*

2. Shells are used to decorate, rather than to cover the whole surface. The color of the box shown is a dark brown. The shells are in the tan tones—calico scallops, arks, bubbles, cockles, with accents of ivory-colored jingles and white arks. Clean your shells, if necessary.

3. Make a paper pattern of the top of the box and arrange the shells on it.

4. Before adding the shells to the box, cover each one with a thin coat of clear nail polish and let them dry.

5. Shells are applied to the top of the box with epoxy cement, using the technique described under "A Mussel Mirror" (Method One), page 56.

Variations

Alternate shells and gold cord or straw braid in a striped pattern.

Cover the box with fine grass or straw cloth—use a placemat—with the edges covered with straw braid, and decorations of shells added to the top and sides, with everything held in place with epoxy cement. This is lovely in its own right, but also solves the problem when your tissue box is an unsatisfying or unmatching color.

DESIGN YOUR OWN BOXES

Three additional boxes using shell motifs are described in two other chapters. See "Stick-on Cache-Pot" in Chapter 5, and in Chapter 6 there is a very interesting slab box or container.

4

Creating Jewelry from the Sea

PENDANTS, necklaces, bracelets, earrings, belts, cuff links are made of shells—all of a kind or mixed varieties. Shells are combined with flat metal, wire, chain, beads, cork or feathers. Or, the shells can be embedded in clear plastic or molded from cold liquid metal. This sort of jewelry, made of shells or rough chunks of coral, is so easy to design and make, while keeping the beautiful, recognizable forms and colors of shells, that you will soon be haunting shell shops and beaches and developing your own designs. The basic techniques needed in jewelry-making are described in this chapter. A number of designs are described in detail, and each one is the basis of a number of new projects.

TOOLS

Some of the designs will need only the simplest tools: *needles* for stringing shells on cord, *toothpicks* for mixing and applying epoxy cement. *Pliers*—either the household variety or jeweler's *chain-nose pliers*—for twisting and bending wire and opening links of chains and jump rings.

For other designs you will need simple jeweler's tools that can be bought in craft shops or by mail order. An *electric soldering iron* or *gun* for applying soft solder. A *jeweler's saw* which is like a hacksaw but has a smaller frame and finer blades. With this you will need a *wooden bench pin* to support the metal to be sawed. Some shells can be bought with

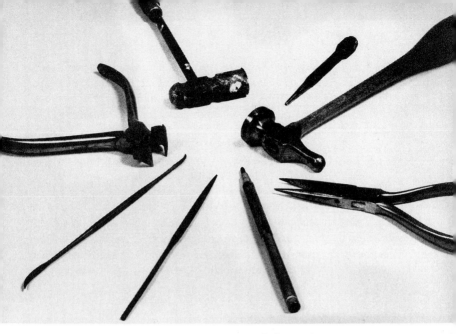

Fig. 65. *Jewelry tools clockwise from top: ballpeen hammer, nail set, planishing hammer, chain-nose pliers, scriber, flat file, riffle file and wire cutter.*

holes already drilled in them, but for others you will need a *hand or electric drill* and fine *drill-bits*.

Other small tools are: *planishing hammer* or *ballpeen hammer*, a *metal file, small wire cutter, scissors* for cutting solder into small squares, a *nail setter*, a *burnisher*, a *metal scriber*, soft *water-color brushes* and possibly a small magnifying glass.

MATERIALS

Shells, first of all, and because each design uses different types of shells, the individual ones will be described at the beginning of each project.

Jewelry *findings* are a must, and these include pinbacks, cuff link backs, earring backs, bellcaps, jump rings and spring catches.

To string shells into necklaces, or to hang as pendants, use *nylon fishing line, linen fishing cord, bead stringing thread or wire, colored cord or yarn, fine wire or link chain*. Brass, copper or *silver wire* can be made into neck wires and hooks to attach pendants to neck wire.

105

For making molds, use *plaster of Paris* or *rubber mold material. Commercial molds* are made of thin plastic, glass and metal. Casting materials include: *clear pouring resin, plastic cooking crystals, cold metal* in tubes, as well as *plaster of Paris.* See Chapters 5 and 6 for directions on the use of molds and molding materials.

Metal soldering supplies are simple. You'll need only *soft solder* in sheet or wire form, *flux,* and a *hard asbestos tile* as a soldering surface. *Paper clips* are a great help in holding things together during soldering. *Rubbing alcohol, powdered kitchen cleanser, cotton* and a *sponge* are all handy when it comes to cleaning metal.

General needs include: *white household glue; epoxy cement; clear nail polish; crocus cloth; masking tape; clear sticky tape; square tile of conglomerate cork, ½-inch thick* to be used when drilling shells; *plasticine* or *plastic putty* (Plasti-Tak) for holding shells steady during working or glue-drying processes.

DRILLING AND SAWING SHELLS

Information on both these processes is fully given at the beginning of Chapter 2.

ANNEALING WIRE

Most wire is very stiff when bought and has to be annealed to make it pliable. Grip the length of wire with pliers, and hold it over the lighted top burner of a gas or electric kitchen stove. Protect the hand holding the pliers with a padded pot holder. Watch the heating carefully so that the wire, especially if silver, does not melt. Have a pot of cold water handy. When the wire is cherry red, drop it into the water. That's all there is to it. If the wire begins to resist you while you are working with it, repeat the annealing process to soften things up.

SOFT SOLDERING TECHNIQUES

Soldering is simply the joining of two pieces of metal by using another metal that melts at a lower temperature, a flux to aid in the melting and a point of contact heat source. The solder used in all the projects in this chapter is a soft solder that melts at the lowest heat. The heat source used is either an electric soldering iron or a gun. For the best control of heat, I prefer the electric soldering gun.

The two pieces of metal to be soldered must be closely fitted together, as the solder will not fill in any gaps, nor will it form a bond unless the two metals are in contact. This fitting operation sometimes takes time and is a matter of careful filing and fitting. At times you may have to use a small magnifying glass to see the joint clearly. Once contact has been established, the next step is to clean the metal.

Any metal to be soldered must be free of all grease, particularly the unseen grease from one's fingers. Wipe the area to be soldered with rubbing alcohol on a piece of absorbent cotton or a powdered kitchen cleanser well-smoothed into a clean wet sponge. Without touching the cleaned surface, hold the metal under running water, then remove. If the surface is covered with a thin film of water, it is perfectly clean. If the water clings as separated drops, clean again as there is still grease on the metal.

Soft solder is sold in thin strips approximately ¾ x 4 inches, or in wire form. After cleaning off the strip to remove any grease, cut 1/16-inch squares, just enough for the project. First cut a 1/16-inch "fringe" along the short side of the solder strip. Make the cuts about ¼ inch deep. If the fringe curls up, flatten with a hammer. Now hold the strip in one hand,

Fig. 66. *Electric soldering gun, soft soldering flux, soft solder (both flat sheet and wire), angled tweezer, fine camel's hair brush and solder scissors.*

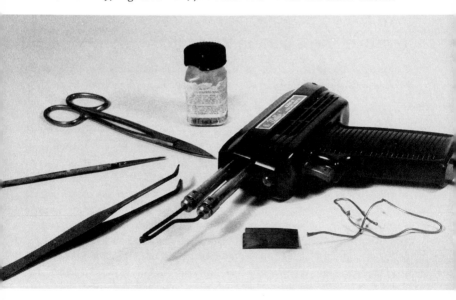

partway down, and place your index finger along the edge of the fringe, then cut as many ⅟₁₆-inch squares as you need, letting them drop on your working surface. Your finger will prevent the small pieces from scattering all over the room.

If you are using soft solder wire, do not buy the acid core type; buy the plain variety of soft solder as you will be adding the right kind of flux. Pound about ½ inch at the end of the wire with a hammer until the wire is flat and thin. Clean off any grease. Cut into ⅟₁₆-inch squares, using the same techniques as for the flat strip.

You are now ready to apply the solder to the area to be joined. Dip a small water-color brush into the liquid flux and apply to the metal joint. Pick up a piece of solder with the wet brush and put it in position at the edge of the joining, or if two wires are crossing each other, then put the solder chip at one side of the cross. Add a little flux on top of the solder and let dry. Heat your iron or gun point and apply at the side *opposite* to the piece of solder, so as to draw the solder under the crack to be joined. The flux will bubble a bit, but keep applying heat until the solder turns shiny and flows. Remove heat immediately and let your object cool. After it is cool, examine carefully to see if you have made a good joining. If not, repeat the process. This can happen to an experienced as well as a beginning craftsperson.

Remove the excess solder with a file, and then smooth the file marks with crocus cloth.

FORMING SOLDERED PRONGS

Many of the shell or coral pendant designs in this chapter are held by wire prongs. These have to be soft-soldered together.

Four Prong Setting

The simplest of all prong settings is made from two pieces of annealed wire crossing each other at right angles and soldered at the center crossing. File a flat notch halfway through the center of two wires after measuring the exact lengths you will need. The notch is just the width of the wire, so that when the notches are placed one over the other there is a flat surface at the joint. The joint is then soldered and the ends turned up over the shell or coral to hold it steady. See "Six Prong Setting" for further details on prong finishing. A jump ring or loop of wire is soldered to the top of the upper prong, or looped over the prong before it is curved over the object. Use the jump ring or the loop to attach the pendant to a chain, cord or neck wire. If you're making a pin, attach a

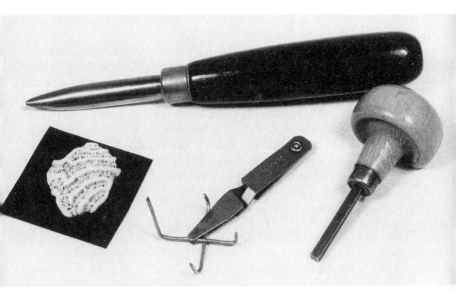

Fig. 67. *Prong, held together with a clip, ready for soft soldering, plus a piece of coral, burnisher and prong setter.*

pinback to the horizontal cross wire. In this case the cross wire should be above the center so the pin won't hang forward.

Six Prong Setting

For larger pieces needing more than four prongs, use a combination of wires and a large jump ring. The jump ring forms the center area to which the prong wires are attached. This spiderlike design is excellent for round or irregularly shaped shells and coral.

To construct the spiderlike support, first place your shell or chunk of coral *face side up* on white paper. Trace around the edge and remove shell. Place the jump ring in the center of the tracing. Measure the six pieces of annealed wire from the edge of the jump ring to the edge of the tracing, allowing enough wire for looping over the ring on one end and turning over the top of your shell or coral on the other end. Cut the wire lengths and place them in position on the tracing.

Now flatten one end of each piece of wire with a ballpeen or planishing hammer. File the edges smooth. With the pliers, curl the flattened end over into a hook. Bring each hook over the jump ring and squeeze each one with the pliers until a tight contact is made between wires and ring. Cut off any excess wire on the hook end.

Dip into rubbing alcohol or rub with powdered kitchen cleanser to remove any grease. Place on the hard asbestos soldering tile. Arrange the wires in their final position, and hold in position with paper clips, if needed. With a small brush place the soft solder flux around each joint. Add a small chip of solder approximately $\frac{1}{16}$-inch square beside the point of the turned-over wire. Apply heat from the soldering gun to each wire on the *inside of the circle*. Remove heat as soon as the solder turns glossy and runs under the wire. Let cool. File all joints smooth, removing any solder or plier marks, even though they will be hidden.

Place your shell or coral on the wire spider, face side up, and mark the bending point of each prong with the scriber. Decide now how you want to finish the ends of the prongs. If you are going to thin out the ends with the hammer, do this while the wires are still flat. Remember that hammering will lengthen the wire, so measure the turnover with a piece of thread to make sure your hammered area will be where you want it, and not be cut off as excess metal. If the ends are to be plain wire filed smooth, then measure the turnover length, cut off excess metal and file off the rough ends. Another finish is to flatten the ends just a bit and split them partway with the solder scissors, then bend the two pieces apart with the pliers to form a double end. A fourth way needs extra long wire prongs, so this one has to be planned from the beginning: the ends are bent into a spiral, which needs anywhere from an extra half-inch to an inch of wire, all depending on the size of the spiral and its proportion to the size of the shell or coral.

Once the ends are finished, you are ready to curve the wires up and over your shell or coral. Make the first right angle bend with your pliers. Do this slowly so you don't put a strain on the metal which could snap if bent too quickly. Slip the shell or coral into the spider to check the fit. If you have a thick piece of coral, mark the next bend on the inside of the wire with the scriber. Remove the coral and bend all the prongs over just a little bit. Again check the fit. Sometimes one bends one or two prongs to their final position to make a firmer hold. Again remove the shell or coral and bend the wires over as far as you can but make sure you're still able to put your shell or coral back into position.

Now add the jump ring to the top prong. You can either solder the jump ring to the prong, or slip the oval jump ring over the prong and back to the first bend. In both cases the hairline opening on the jump ring should be soldered for a firmer hold. This is also the time to solder on a pinback, picking a matching spot on two of the upper angled wires, well above center.

File away any plier marks, and polish wires with crocus cloth before putting your object in place for the final setting of the prongs.

Place coral in position and smooth the wires over with the burnisher, starting at the edge and working inward. Always work on opposite wires, never wires in progression around the circle, or you will find your piece out of alignment.

A thinner-edge shell is handled in the same way, except that after the first right-angled bend you will continue the bend of the prong with just enough curve-over to fit the shell.

If the prongs do not lie absolutely flat, you may have to tap them down gently with a nail-set and hammer.

Work from the outside to the end of each prong, and be very careful not to crack the shell.

VARIATION 1: You can also use half-round wire instead of round or square wire. The flat side of the half-round rests against your object.

VARIATION 2: If you are making a prong setting for a long narrow shell, first cut the vertical wire and, instead of a single horizontal cross wire, plan on two cross wires. Proceed as you did in the "Four Prong Setting."

OPENING JUMP RINGS

Jump rings are commercially-made rings of copper, silver or gold-filled wire in several sizes from less than 1/8 inch to 3/8 inch. They are round, oval or triangular in shape. The joint is unsoldered. To open, grasp the wire on each side of the joint with two pairs of pliers, one on each side. Pull apart *sideways,* just wide enough to slip in another ring or chain link. Never pull apart by just widening the space between the wires, as this will distort the ring's shape. Close by bringing the wire back into position with the ends tight together. If you need extra strength to support a heavy piece of coral, shell or chain, the joint can be soldered in the closed position.

NECK WIRE

This is a modern and very useful holder for a pendant, and it is extremely easy to make. The average neck wire is 5 inches in diameter, but measure your own neck with a piece of heavy carpet thread. Cut it

Fig. 68. *Pounding the end of the neck wire to form the fastening hook.*

Fig. 69. *Curling the hook over with chain-nose pliers.*

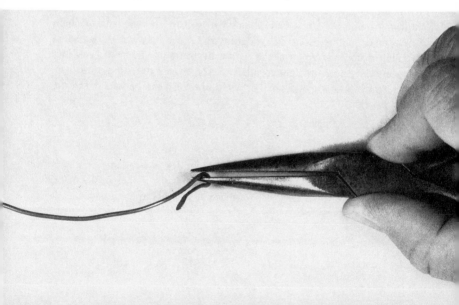

off at the joining and stretch out the thread on your working surface. Put a length of 18-gauge silver or brass wire beside it, allowing an extra ½ inch at each end of the wire for the fastening hooks. Cut wire.

Bend the wire around a coffee or paint can to achieve a smooth circle, bringing the ends across each other so that there will be no flat areas and the wire will be under tension.

With the round end of a ballpeen hammer, pound ⅜ inch on each end of the wire to form a narrow oval. File the ends smooth and go over the surface with crocus cloth. Curl the ends over into a hook, using chain-nose pliers. Bring the ends close to the wire. File off any plier marks, and give the whole surface a final polish with the crocus cloth before covering the surface with clear nail polish to prevent tarnishing.

EMBEDDING SHELLS IN PLASTIC

Information on this process is fully given at the beginning of Chapter 5. The various embedding methods can be used for pendants, earrings and pins, and such designs will be described later in this chapter.

COLD METAL CASTING

One can approximate silver metal by using one of several liquid, cold solders available in tubes at hardware or craft stores. When these materials are squeezed into a rubber or silicone mold (see beginning of Chapter 6 for directions) and are allowed to harden, the result is surprisingly close. You have been saved both the high cost of raw material plus the equipment needed for hot metal casting. This is one of the advantages of modern technology for the home craftsperson.

The hardened metal can be smoothed with crocus cloth, and for a bright finish add a coat of clear nail polish. Another method is to mix aluminum powder into clear pouring resin.

A TURRET PENDANT

This is the simplest of all pendants to make. A Turret Shell—either *Turritella exoleta, terebra* or *variegata*—is hung from a black or colored cord. It is very effective. I've seen these designs in shops in Puerto Rico.

Tools and Materials

Scissors, ruler and toothpicks plus a metal skewer are all the tools needed.

A Turret Shell, which is narrow, pointed, whorled and up to 3 inches in length in tones of ivory, tan and brown. A length of cord long enough to go around the neck and hang down in front, plus ½ inch at each end. Epoxy cement.

Steps

1. Clean and prepare shell, if necessary.
2. Mix epoxy cement. (See page 43.)
3. Put two drops of epoxy cement into the opening of the Turret Shell. Cover ⅜ to ½ inch of cord at each end with epoxy cement, and then stuff the ends into the top opening of the shell using a thin metal meat skewer.
4. Add more cement at the opening to soak into the cord and onto the shell. Let dry for 24 hours. Check the holding power of the glue. You may want to add another coat at the top of the opening. Let it dry. And that's all there is to it.

SPIRAL PENDANT

One of the simplest pendants is made from a black or pearly Turban or Top Shell (*Turbo,* or *Cittarium*), or a green Snail Shell (*Papuina pulcherrime*) or any other peaked shell with deep grooves, plus a length of gleaming brass wire which is wrapped around the curved whorls of the shells. Very elegant and understated.

Tools and Materials

Only two tools are needed: pliers and a metal file. For variations, add a toothpick and a hammer.

A pointed Snail Shell of wearable size, as a pendant. Brass wire, 20- to 22-gauge, but the thickness and length does depend on the size of the shell. A spool of carpet thread, one or more oval jump rings and a length of chain. Ring catch, if chain is a short one. Crocus cloth, epoxy cement and clear nail polish.

Steps

1. Clean the shell, if necessary. Measure the length of wire needed by wrapping a piece of thread around the channel of the shell, allowing

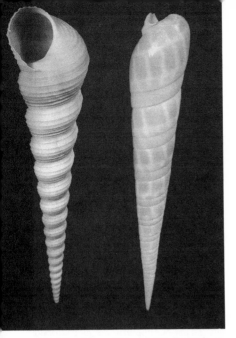

FIG. 70. *Two Turret Shells* (Turritella terebra cerea) *from the Pacific and an orange-colored Turret Shell.*

FIG. 71.
Simple turret pendant
showing the attachment
of shell to cord.

FIG. 72. *Two Turban or Top-type Shells, the one on the left with the outer skin removed, plus the green Pacific* Papuina pulcherrime.

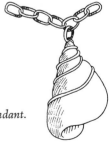

FIG. 73. *The finished spiral pendant.*

enough for a small hanging circle at the top and a hook at the bottom.

2. Anneal the wire so it bends easily around the shell. (See page 106.)

3. With a hammer, pound ⅜ inch at one end of the wire so that it becomes flat and thin. File edges smooth. Make a close-fitting hook of the wire. Slip the hook over a convenient part of the shell's wide opening, with the short end of the hook inside.

4. Now, using your fingers and the pliers, bring the wire up and around the shell, following the spiral groove.

5. When you reach the top of the shell, curl the wire over with the pliers to form a circle.

6. Open an oval jump ring, insert the top circle and also the center link of the chain. Close the jump ring. If you want your pendant to dangle from the chain, add as many jump rings as you need.

7. If the whorls of the shell are shallow, you may want to add a thin coat of epoxy cement between the wire and the shell to hold everything in place. Let dry undisturbed for 24 hours.

8. Take out any marks made by the pliers, using the metal file and the crocus cloth. Protect the shell with strips of typewriter paper slipped under the wire. Cover wire with clear nail polish, again protecting the shell with strips of paper. Do not allow the paper to stick to the nail polish.

Word of warning. If you are working with a thin shell, partly form the wire into a spiral, then slip over the shell and tighten. This way, you'll avoid too much pressure on the shell.

Variation

Instead of a circle at the top of the shell, bring 1½ inches of wire up above the point, flatten about ¼ inch of wire at the end and turn over to form a hook. Hang hook and shell from a neck wire. (See page 111.)

A CORD FULL OF COWRIES

A large, white-patterned brown cowrie is hung as a pendant from a cord decorated with small cowries, making the wearer feel part of a warm tropical scene.

Tools and Materials

Scissors, ruler, fine felt-tipped pen, skewer, needle and toothpicks will do the job for you.

A large, Measled Cowrie (*Cypraea exanthema* or *zebra*), about 2½ to 3 inches long. Approximately 20 small white cowries, or Coffee Bean

Fig. 74. *An assortment of cowries and trivias.*

Trivia (*Trivia pediculus*) which are pink shells with brown spots (very much like a cowrie) ¼ to ½ inches long. This is where the Latin name is very important, as there is another shell whose common name is Coffee Bean Shell (*Melampus coffeus*) which is actually quite different. The number of shells will depend on their size and the necklace length. Round black or colored cord and a ring catch and jump ring if the necklace is too short to go over the head. Plastic putty, Plasti-Tak, or plasticene. Epoxy cement, toothpicks, string and thread.

Steps

1. Clean shells, if necessary. Measure the length of cord you will need by holding a piece of string around your neck. For a long necklace, the two ends of the cord will be epoxied along the length of the cowrie opening, so allow enough extra cord at each end.

2. Mix epoxy cement. Coat the sides of the opening in the shell, and also coat the two ends of the cord the same length as the shell opening. Put a piece of plastic putty or plasticene on your working surface, and press the curved outside of the shell into it so the shell is held steady. With the skewer, stuff the cord ends along the shell's seam, keeping them side by side.

117

3. Let the cord and cowrie dry undisturbed for 24 hours.

4. Add a second layer of epoxy, spreading it over the top of the two short lengths of cord and running over onto the shell. Again let dry for 24 hours.

5. Now plan your design for the rest of the necklace. With the cowrie still supported, spread out the cord in a wide loop over your working surface which should be protected with newspaper.

6. The first cluster of small shells will be attached to the cord at a point beginning 1 inch from the large pendant shell. Make a mark on the newspaper right beside the cord at this 1-inch spot. Place four small cowries or Coffee Bean Trivia end to end on the newspaper beside the cord, stretching away from the center shell. Repeat on the other side.

7. Measure off 2 inches on each side and again make a mark on the newspaper. Place two shells end to end beginning at this mark and working toward the center back. Repeat on the other side.

8. Next, measure off 2 inches and place four shells end to end. Repeat on other side.

9. Continue this pattern until you reach the center back of the cord.

10. Place strips of plastic putty under the cord in each area where the shells will be attached to the cord.

11. Mix epoxy cement. Lift up cord and place the first cluster of shells on the plastic putty, rounded side down. Smear epoxy over the top of the shells and on the underside of the cord, and press both together, poking the cord slightly into the opening of each shell, but not too deeply as you do not want any kinks in it. Continue with each cluster until all shells have been cemented in position. Let dry for 24 hours. Add a second coat of epoxy over the cord and down onto the shells. Let dry again for 24 hours. And the necklace is ready to wear.

Variation

1. If you are making a short necklace, the large cowrie pendant will be attached to a center *loop* of cord, the length of the opening in the shell. Attach with epoxy cement following the directions in Steps 2 to 4.

2. Turn over ½ inch of cord at each end and hold in place with thread. Sew through the double thickness of cord along the ½-inch length, then wrap the thread around the two thicknesses in a tight spiral. Finish off the thread with a loop knot, cut off thread and bury the end in the center of the cord. Sew a jump ring on the end of one side and the ring catch on the other.

3. Add the small white cowries or Coffee Bean Trivia in a pattern, following directions in Steps 5 to 11.

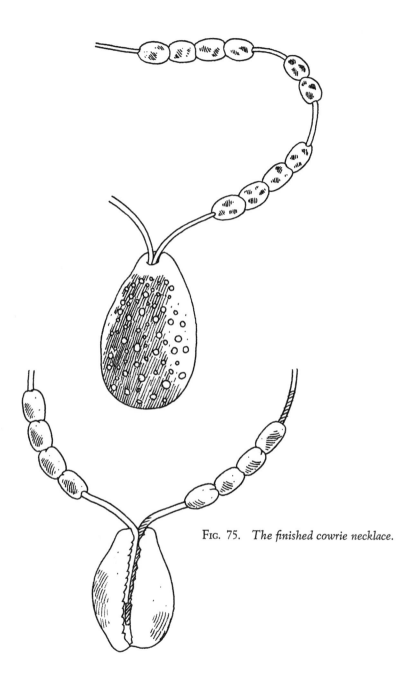

Fig. 75. *The finished cowrie necklace.*

SHELL FRINGE PENDANT

Small shells, all one type or mixed varieties, are hung on short lengths of clear nylon fishing line, and each line is attached to a notch on a 2½-inch bar of square wire, made of brass or silver. This barbaric fringe is hung from a neck wire or chain. Cut bar to size from longer piece of wire.

Tools and Materials

For this project you will need a jeweler's saw, metal file, pliers, wire cutter, soldering iron or gun, ballpeen hammer, scissors and toothpicks. The number of shells needed depends on the size of the shells and the size of the pendant you want to make. Try using black-and-white Zebra Nerite (*Purperita pupa*), or Checkered Nerite (*Nerita tessellata*), small cowries or pink Coffee Bean (*Trivia*), small cones or olives, Black Horn Shells (*Batillaria minima*) or periwinkles. A 2½-inch bar of square wire in brass or silver, just under ⅛-inch square. A 4½-inch length of 18-gauge silver or brass wire. Clear nylon fishing line, 20 pound test. Soft

FIG. 76. *Black-and-white Nerite Shells.*

solder and flux, asbestos tile, crocus cloth and powdered kitchen cleanser. Epoxy cement, plasticene or Plasti-Tak, sticky tape, clear nail polish and paper clips.

Steps

1. All the metal work will be completed first. To begin with, file five triangular notches into the top surface of the square metal bar, beginning ¼ inch in from the left side and making a notch every ½ inch. You should end up with the last notch ¼ inch in from the right side. The notches are about $\frac{1}{16}$ inch deep.

2. Smooth out any nicks or surface marks on the metal with crocus cloth.

3. Cut the 4½-inch length of wire in half with the wire cutter. Pound one end of each wire into a thin oval, ¼ inch in from one end, tapping and stretching the metal with the rounded end of the hammer. File the edges into a smooth oval and polish with the crocus cloth.

4. With the pliers, bend each pounded end over into a hook. These ends will slip over the neck wire or chain.

5. As these wires will be soldered to the ends of the bar, angling in a bit, check the length by holding the bar and wires against the neck wire or chain. You might temporarily hold the wires in place on the bar with sticky tape. Cut off any excess wire.

6. Slightly flatten the ends to be soldered to make a better contact.

7. Wash off wires and bar with powdered kitchen cleanser to remove all grease.

8. With the notches at the top, decide which side looks best and place this side face downward on the soldering-tile surface, with the notches away from you.

9. Put the ends of each wire on the back surface of the bar between the end and the first notch, pointing away from you. The slightly flattened end of each wire is in contact with the bar, and the hooks face downward. The wires should slant toward each other at a 60° angle. Hold each wire in position with a paper clip.

10. Add flux and solder chips, and heat with the electric soldering gun. (See soldering, page 106.)

11. Clean and prepare the shells, if necessary. Then go on to make the shell fringe. The first step is to pat or roll out a 3-inch square of plastic putty or plasticene. Put it on your working surface, and use the skewer to draw in grooves, ½ inch apart, as guides for the shells.

12. Press shells lightly into the grooves with their openings facing up, allowing a little space between them. You will now have the pattern of

the five fringes of vertically hanging shells with their "viewing" side embedded in the putty.

13. Make a knot at the end of the nylon line. Starting at the bottom shell of one fringe, measure up to the bar, and then allow enough extra line to go over the bar twice and return halfway down the first shell. Cut off line. Repeat four more times, always starting with a knot, until you have five cut lines.

14. Mix epoxy cement. Spread it into the opening of each shell on the first fringe. Tuck the knot into the bottom of the opening of the first shell, carry the line up the shell to the next one and so on up the full length of the shells. Let the excess line dangle. Repeat on all lines of shells. Let dry undisturbed for 24 hours.

15. Add a second thin coat of epoxy over the nylon line, spreading it out onto the shells. Let dry again for 24 hours.

16. Put the bar in position across the line of shells, ¼ inch above the top shells. The hook side faces downward and the soldered side faces you. Bring the free end of the line under the bar, over the notch, across the back, down and under, and across the notch again. Make a small knot, holding the end of the line to the supporting line, then bring the free end down to the back of the top shell. Do this with all five lines. You may feel all thumbs, but if you tape each line against the top shell the process will be easier.

17. When all five lines are secured, remove tape and tuck the end of each line into a shell opening, cutting off any excess line. Add epoxy cement to hold ends in position. Dry for 24 hours. Add a second coat of epoxy if needed.

18. Carefully remove the shells from the putty when all is hard and dry. Remove any putty from the shells with rubbing alcohol. (But this should not happen, as the shells were only balanced in it to hold them steady.) And your pendant is now ready to be hooked onto a neckwire or chain.

Variations

Four cowries to a string, and a small Cone Shell on the end. Three Olive Shells to a string, and a cowrie at the end. In place of nylon fishing line, use nylon bead-stringing cord or fine bead-stringing wire, or very fine metal chain. In the case of wire, bring it over the notch only once and wrap free end around the facing wire between the bar and the top shell, then tuck the end of the wire into the shell opening and hold with epoxy cement.

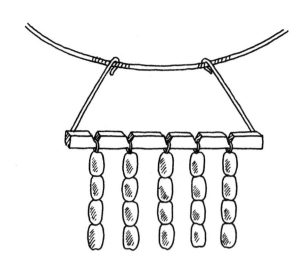

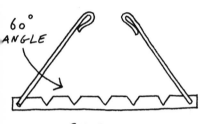

60°
ANGLE

REVERSE SIDE

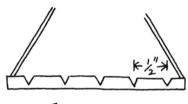

½"

FRONT SIDE

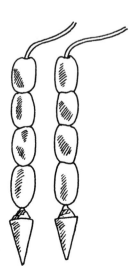

Fig. 77. Diagrams of finished shell fringe pendant, Step 9 diagrams, fringe variations.

FIG. 78. *Rare color form of the Netted Olive* (Olivia reticularis).

PRONGED SHELL PENDANTS

Large, spectacular shells are held by metal prongs—either four or six prongs—then hung by a hook from a neck wire or chain.

The shell used in this project is a rare color form of the Netted Olive (*Olivia reticularis*), of which only a few have been found. I found two specimens on a beach in St. Lucia, West Indies. I have kept one, and the other I gave to Dr. William K. Emerson of the American Museum of Natural History in New York who made the identification for me. This one is banded in deep burnt orange and ivory—a beautiful and precious shell.

Tools and Materials

Soldering tools—iron or gun; fine brush, pliers, wire cutter, metal file, burnisher, nail-set and hammer, metal scriber and paper clips.

Shells—Miter (*Mitra*), Cone (*Conus*), Spiny Murex (*Murex ternispina*), Olive (*Oliva textilina*), Thorny Oyster (*Spondylus regius*) are other choices. Silver or brass 18-gauge wire for the prongs; the amount needed depends on the size of the shell. You can use round, half-round or square wire. Neck wire or chain, solder and flux, powdered kitchen cleanser and crocus cloth. Asbestos tile, clear nail polish, jump ring and perhaps a ring catch.

Steps

1. Clean the shell, if necessary. With a piece of fine wire or thread, measure your shell for the amount of silver or brass wire you will need for your prongs. The long shells should have two prongs on each side and one at each end. A large, roundish shell needs the spider type of prong setting.

2. Cut the wire into the proper lengths, clean, solder and form the prongs. (See page 108.)

3. Make a wire hook, following directions given on page 130, steps 3 and 4 (illustration page 129). Add to the top prong before bending it into the final position. Or add jump ring.

4. Place the shell in position and bend prongs inward to grip the upper surface of the shell.

5. Cover all metal surfaces with clear nail polish to prevent tarnishing.

Variation

If the shell is very pointed at top or bottom or both, plan to split and spread both ends of the vertical wire so that it grips the shell on each side of the point. Or, form a loop at each end of the wire into which the point can snuggle.

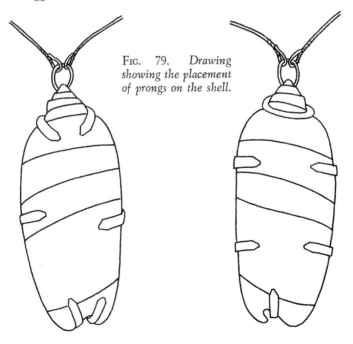

FIG. 79. *Drawing showing the placement of prongs on the shell.*

A WHIRLIGIG PENDANT

Several Ram's Horns or Common Spirulas (*Spirula spirula*) are made into a circular design with a limpet in the middle—the whole thing resting on a circle of metal or plastic. The ram's horn is the inside thin, white "shell" of a floating Cephalopod. They are about 1 inch across and are found in Florida and Puerto Rico and on other southern beaches.

Tools and Materials

Drill, pliers, file, hammer and nail (optional) and toothpicks.

A 2½ to 3 inch circle of brass, pewter or aluminum. As an alternate base, plastic cooking crystals and a mold. Five or six Ram's Horns, depending on size. One Keyhole Limpet (*Diodora*) for the center of the design. Oval jump ring, chain, crocus cloth and powdered kitchen cleanser, epoxy cement, toothpick, and clear nail polish.

Steps

1. Near the edge of the circle drill a hole large enough to hold the oval jump ring. If you're using aluminum, you can make the hole with a nail and hammer.

2. Hold the metal circle in one hand with the outside facing up. File the edge at a 45° angle. This will optically thicken it and add a slanting, shining edge which turns a plain piece of metal into jewelry.

3. Polish the metal circle with the crocus cloth, taking out any scratches or nicks. Remove any grease with powdered kitchen cleanser.

4. Clean and prepare the shells, if necessary. Arrange the shells in a

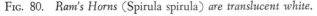

Fɪɢ. 80. *Ram's Horns* (Spirula spirula) *are translucent white.*

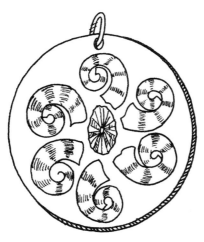

FIG. 81. *Brass and shell pendant.*

design with the curved part of the Ram's Horns on the outer edge. Fill in the middle space with the Keyhole Limpet.

5. Mix the epoxy cement and attach the shells to the metal in this manner: Cover the underside of a shell with epoxy cement, press onto the metal, lift up and add a thin layer of epoxy over the impression. Re-epoxy the shell and place in position. Repeat with each shell. After all shells are in place let dry for 24 hours. Check shells to see if any more epoxy is needed around edges.

6. Cover exposed metal with an even coat of clear nail polish to prevent tarnishing. Let dry for 12 hours.

7. Slip a jump ring through the hole at the top and attach it to a chain.

Variation

1. An alternate method is to fill a shallow round mold with plastic crystals and put it in the oven to partially melt them. (See Chapter 5 for complete directions on the use of this material.)

2. Pull mold to the front of the oven and quickly put the shells in position and close oven door until the plastic is completely melted. The shells will sink partway into the material, and will be held firmly in place.

3. Take out, cool, and remove from the mold. When completely cool, drill or use a hot nail to make a hole for the jump ring, add it, then hang on a chain.

127

ST. LUCIA ON A CHAIN

This design is based on a piece of coral ⅝ inch thick and 2½ inches long and is held with metal prongs and hung on a chain or neck wire. By chance, as I wandered along the beach at St. Lucia searching for shells, I found a piece of coral in the shape of the island. After soaking it in Clorox water and taking off a few flat red spots of coral, it became a lacy, creamy jewel. Flat coral found on island beaches is fascinating with its many different designs and shapes—and one swoops down on each nugget with joy, seeing a new design in each find.

Tools and Materials

Soldering iron or gun, file, wire cutter, pliers, ballpeen or planishing hammer, burnisher and metal scriber.

A piece of coral suitable for a pendant. Twenty-gauge brass or silver wire for pendant support and prongs. Asbestos tile, soft solder and flux. Crocus cloth and powdered kitchen cleanser, clear nail polish, chain or neck wire.

FIG. 82. *Coral in the shape of St. Lucia in the West Indies.*

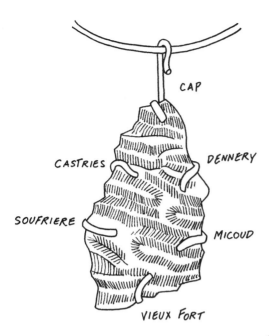

CAP

CASTRIES

DENNERY

SOUFRIERE

MICOUD

VIEUX FORT

FIG. 83. *Coral turned into a pendant with prongs and hanging hook.*

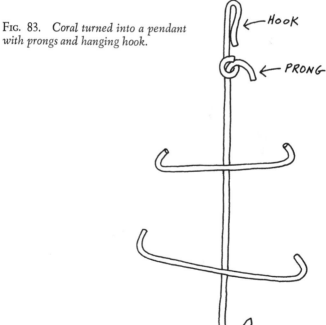

HOOK

PRONG

Steps

1. Clean and prepare the coral, if necessary.

2. Here are the steps for making the St. Lucia pendant, but this design can be followed for any coral that is longer than it is wide. Only the measurements of the wire prongs and supports will change.

3. Make an outline of the coral on thin paper, and mark the areas along the edges where the prongs will look best. Next, measure on the coral with heavy thread to find the length for each prong—across the back, up the sides and over onto the front.

4. Cut the half-round wire (you can use round or square wire) into four lengths; mine are 3⅝ inches for the vertical back support, 2⅞ inches for the lower horizontal support, 2¼ inches for the upper horizontal support, and 1¾ to 2 inches for the attached hook, which will hold the pendant to a chain or neck wire.

5. Turn the tracing over so that you're working on the "back" of the coral. Put the vertical wire in position, flat side down so the two ends are in the right position to turn over the thickness of the coral.

6. Put the two crosspieces in position and mark the crossing areas with the scriber on the horizontal and vertical wires.

7. File notches so the wires will fit into each other. Smooth out any nicks or surface marks with crocus cloth. Finish the prong ends, solder and turn up the prongs. (See page 108.)

8. To make the hanging hook, cut a 1¾-to 2-inch length of 20-gauge brass or silver wire. Pound one end of the wire into a thin oval, ¼ inch in from one end, tapping and stretching the metal with the rounded end of a hammer. File the edges into a smooth oval and polish with the crocus cloth.

9. With the pliers, bend the end over into a hook so that the flat oval area touches the straight wire. Curl the other end into a tight circle, using the point of the chain-nose pliers. File off any marks and polish with crocus cloth.

10. Slip the round circle over the top prong before completing the prong bending onto the front of the coral.

11. Complete the bending over of the prongs, cover all metal with clear nail polish to prevent tarnishing—and your island pendant is ready to wear.

AN ABALONE TURTLE

The changing greens and blues of Abalone Shell (*Haliotis*) shine through the crossed wires of this turtle's back. It can be a very simple, no-soldering pendant—or, following the "variation" directions, it can have soldered cross wires over the flat shell.

Tools and Materials

Drill, soldering tools, jeweler's saw, wire cutter, file, pliers, burnisher and scriber.

A flat, oval piece of Abalone Shell, 2 inches long. A piece of aluminum, brass, pewter or silver 2 x 3 inches, 18-gauge. A length of half-round brass or silver wire, 9 inches long. Jump ring or wire for hook. Crocus cloth, rubbing alcohol or powdered kitchen cleanser, carbon paper.

Steps

1. If you cannot buy the suggested size of shell, adapt the design to whatever is available. Make a tracing of the shell on a sheet of paper. Put a sheet of thin tracing paper over the shell outline and copy the turtle design.

2. Transfer your design to the metal with carbon paper. The outer edge of metal is a hair's breadth wider than the shell. The inner edge is ⅛ to ³⁄₁₆ inches in from the outer edge. The flat prongs are along the outer edge as flaps which will be bent under to hold the shell, for all the world like the flaps on paperdoll dresses.

3. Remove the pattern and trace over the carbon line with the metal scriber. Wipe off the metal with rubbing alcohol to remove the carbon line.

4. Drill a hole for the saw blade, and with the jeweler's saw cut out the interior metal. Then cut around the outside edge. File the edges smooth, angling the edge as you file to create a thicker look. Polish it with crocus cloth. (See pages 40 and 42.)

5. Drill a hole for the oval jump ring.

6. Put the metal turtle outline face downward on the working surface. Place the Abalone Shell in position with the colorful side against the frame. Now bend the eight prongs over the shell, always bending opposite prongs in succession, never going around from one to the next. Bend each one partway down, and then go around again, repeating the progression of opposite prongs. Bring all prongs down tightly against the shell.

FIG. 84. *A section of Abalone Shell* (Haliotis).

7. Go over the metal again with crocus cloth to remove any scratches that developed during the setting of the shell. Then coat metal with clear nail polish to prevent it from tarnishing.

Variations

This design involves soldering six crossing wires over the "back" of the turtle, through which the Abalone Shell will show. One method is simple, the other a bit more complicated.

1. Solder both ends of three of the wires to the underside of the frame, working with the underside of the frame facing you. The curved side of the half-round wire is facing away from you. Then lay the other three wires over the first three, crossing at an angle, and solder at the sides. Clean and polish. And set prongs as in Steps 6 and 7. (See page 106.)

2. Solder the first three wires as above. Then notch both this set and the other three wires at the crossing points so that they fit smoothly together. Solder both the ends and the crossing points of the second set of three wires. Clean wires, and set prongs.

132

Fig. 85. *Diagram of metal frame and fold-over prongs (above), plus variation (below).*

Fig. 86. *An assortment of narrow shells found on southern beaches.*

SPIKY NECKLACE

String the pointed, bumpy or smooth shells found on all beaches into a spiky necklace. Most of the shells are 1 to 1¼ inches long, ¼ to ⅜ inches wide at the top, and are variously Horn (*Cerithidea*), Screw (*Terebra*), Miter (*Mitra*) Shells in shades of gray, tan and brown. There are a number of species in each genus. Once in a while you'll find longer Turret Shells (*Turritella*), so use these as center accents.

Tools and Materials

Drill, pliers and scissors are all you need.

Shells—the number depends on the length of the necklace and the size of the shells. And the length of the necklace depends on how many shells you've gathered—sort of like the chicken and the egg. But that is the fun of working with natural things hand-gathered; there are no hard and fast formulas sometimes. Nylon fishing line, 20 pound test, or nylon bead-stringing thread. Ring catch and jump ring.

134

Steps

1. Clean and prepare the shells, if necessary. Drill a small hole in the flared part of the opening of each shell. (See page 40.)

2. String the shells on the nylon line.

3. If the length is too short to go over your head, tie one end of the line to a ring catch and the other to a jump ring.

4. If the necklace will go over your head, tie the two ends firmly together and your necklace is finished.

Variation

With all the shell necklaces a pendant of a larger shell can be added, or even several larger shells across the front of the necklace, with perhaps two shells in the center, one below the other hung on jump rings.

FIG. 87. *Long narrow shells strung into a necklace.*

PINK SHELL NECKLACE

A double chain looking like a Hawaiian lei is made of Rosy Carnara Shells (*Strigilla carnaria*) which are white on the outside and deep pink inside; these range from ¾ to 1 inch wide. I've found the shells on the beaches of Puerto Rico and St. Lucia and also along the eastern coast from the Carolinas southward. Often you will find them with a single hole at the top which cuts down on your own drilling time. The hole was made by a gastropod—a drill—looking for a meal.

Tools and Materials

Drill and pliers are all you need in the way of tools.

Approximately 60 shells for a short necklace, and 76 or more for an over-the-head necklace. If you cannot find the rosy carnara, you can substitute Rose Petal (*Tellina lineata*) or Watermelon Tellins (*Tellina punicae*). Thin nylon fishing line, 10-pound test, or nylon bead-stringing thread. Ring catch and jump ring for a short necklace.

Steps

1. Clean and prepare the shells, if necessary. Drill two holes in each shell—one at the point and one in the center of the shell. If the shell has a hole at the point, drill only the one in the center. (See page 40.)

2. Nylon fishing line is stiff so you will not need a needle. Poke the end of the line through the top hole from the outside, down the inside, and out through the middle hole. Hold the next shell with the inside of the shell facing up and bring the line through the hole at the point and then through the middle hole. Hold next shell with curved side up against the curved part of the last shell, bring the line through the hole at the top, down the inside and out through the middle hole—and so on until all the shells are used, or the necklace is the length you want it to be. Shells are always back to back, that is, the curved surfaces are always against each other and the pink inside facing outward on both sides. It is best to work on a flat surface with the shells left on the working area and the nylon line still attached to the spool, so that you can keep pulling on the line as you need it.

3. When the necklace is complete or nearly so, try it against your neck for length. If this is a short necklace, attach the catch to one end of the line and snip off excess thread. Pull the shells as tightly together as you wish. They should lie flat against each other in two rows, the back of one shell in the space between the backs of two other shells. Once the

Fig. 88. *Rosy Carnara Shells* (Strigilla carnaria) *strung together for a necklace.*

tension is right and not so tight that the necklace will buckle, tie on the jump ring and cut off excess line.

4. If the necklace is long enough to go over your head, you will not need to add a catch. Tighten the shells and tie both ends of the line together, then trim off the extra line.

Variation

Use this design for a bracelet.

BARBARIC JEWEL OF A NECKLACE

Pieces of Abalone Shell, a large chunk of coral, some hishi made from sea shells or ostrich egg shells, sea beans, a few trading beads, long narrow shells, small cork balls from fishing tackle, all spaced out with short brass tubes and hung on a fine metal chain.

Tools and Materials

Pliers, scissors, wire cutter, file and soldering equipment.

All the shell material listed above, or your own combination of shells, and hishi—¾ inch circles cut from ostrich shells—measuring 15 to an inch. The center pendant can be a 2- to 3-inch shell or coral that is wrapped with wire to eliminate any soldering. A narrow, gold-filled chain. The brass tubes are "sleeves" used in fishing tackle and can be bought at sporting goods stores. Solder and flux. Crocus cloth, clear nail polish, spring catch and jump ring.

Steps

1. Clean and prepare the shells, if necessary. Start with a flat chunk of coral—mine is a heart-shaped piece from a beach in Puerto Rico. Add a spider support of brass or silver wire plus a jump ring. (See page 108.)

2. String the chain through the jump ring at the top of the coral pendant.

3. Drill holes, ¼ inch from the top of the Abalone Shell pieces. Also drill a hole in the top of each Turret or Horn Shell, if you are using them.

4. Polish the brass tubes with crocus cloth. Coat with clear nail polish to keep from tarnishing.

5. Now start stringing everything together. A sleeve on each side of the coral. Then eight hishi, a sleeve, a long pointed shell, a sleeve, eight hishi, a sleeve, Abalone Shell piece, a sleeve, eight hishi, a sleeve, sea bean or bead. If you feel it is too heavy, leave the chain bare from the shoulder area or before. End up with a small bright bead as this will not slip over either the catch or jump ring at the end of the chain. You can also tie the chain into a knot that is bigger than the hole in the last hishi. This will keep the arrangement from sliding. This whole arrangement is a matter of balancing shells and objects properly in relation to your neck, height and a comfortable wearing weight.

6. Add the catch and jump ring at either end of the chain. Wear the necklace for fun and the memory of a tropical beach.

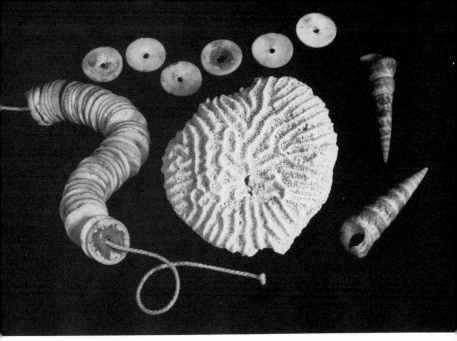

Fig. 89. *Variegated Turret Shells* (Turritella variegata), *a piece of coral and Ostrich Shell Hishi.*

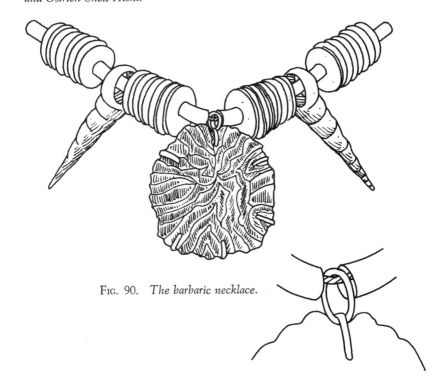

Fig. 90. *The barbaric necklace.*

BROWN SPIRALS

Brown spiral shells seem to spin around on a necklace. They are Tree Snail Shells from the trees along the beach in Puerto Rico, and their brown-and-ivory colors make an elegant short necklace.

Tools and Materials

Drill, pliers and a wire cutter will make the project.

Approximately 12 brown-and-ivory Tree Snails, 1¼ inches wide, will be needed, plus a small-link chain of choker length. Ring catch and jump ring to finish off the chain. Also 12 jump rings to hold the shells in position on the chain.

Steps

1. Clean and prepare the shells, if necessary.

2. Measure your neck for the right necklace length with a piece of string. Cut off the end and stretch the string flat on your working surface. Arrange the shells along the string, leaving several inches at each end free of shells.

3. Now put the chain beside the string and move shells and jump rings around until the jump rings match the links. Remember that when the necklace is worn, the jump rings will slide down to the front corner of each link—so plan accordingly.

4. Drill a small hole just below the outside center of the shell aperture. Make it large enough to hold the oval jump ring. Repeat the drilling with the rest of the shells. (See page 40.)

5. Open jump rings and slip each one through the hole in a shell, and then through its link in the chain. Close jump rings.

6. Hold the chain against your neck for a final check of the length, remove a link or two if necessary. Add the ring catch and jump ring, one at each end of the chain. If the links are solid, with no break for an opening, you'll have to attach the catch with a separate jump ring. Remember that rings and catch add extra length to your necklace, so plan accordingly.

ORANGE SCALLOP BIB

This is a variation of the Brown Spirals design. Orange Scallop Shells form a glowing bib necklace. Use Rough Scallops (*Pecten* or *Acquipectin muscosus*) which are up to 2 inches long and are found on the southeastern coast of the United States and in the West Indies.

Tools and Materials

You will need the same tools as in the previous project—drill, pliers and wire cutter.

Orange Scallop Shells, approximately 1⅜ inches wide. Fine chain, oval jump rings and ring catch. The number of rings and shells will depend on the size of the shells.

Steps

1. Clean and prepare shells, if necessary.
2. Follow directions for measuring the length of the necklace and drilling shells, as given under "Brown Spirals" (Steps 1 to 4).
3. Space out the shells to allow a ¼-inch space between the widest part of each shell. After attaching the shells by jump rings to the chain, add a "chain" made of jump rings between the five front shells to hold a second row of four shells which will hang from these four jump ring chains. (See Fig. 94.) The tops of the shells will just clear the bottoms of the first row of shells—so you can see why all depends on the size of the shells.
4. Finish necklace with ring catch and jump ring.

THE PRIMITIVE WORLD

Shells and other assorted decorations are all hung on a ¼-inch-in-diameter piece of hemp rope, either natural color or stained. The finished necklace projects the mood of a line of flotsam cast up from the sea on a hot, tropical beach. Look in museums or primitive art books for ideas for this and other necklace variations.

Tools and Materials

Pliers, scissors, a drill and toothpicks will be needed.

Scrounge around for bright feathers, tufts of fiber from coconut husks, Australian pine needles (found near southern beaches), trading beads, Turkey Wing Shells (*Arca occidentalis*), pieces of broken shells in interesting shapes. On southern island beaches you will find broken Top-Shells (*Cittarium pica*) which show the pearly inside surface, or the shiny, bright pink inside surface of Helmet Shells (*Cassis*), or Queen Conch (*Strombus gigas*). Use a Scotch Bonnet (*Phalium granulatum*) or some other spectacular shell for a center pendant. Many Indian Craft mail order houses have feathers and bright quills listed in their catalogs.

Fig. 91. *Tree Snail Shell from Puerto Rico.*

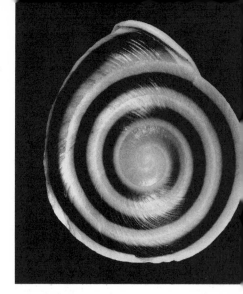

Fig. 95. *Turkey Wing* (Arca occidentalis) *from Florida.*

142

FIG. 92. Brown-and-ivory Tree Snails hung on a chain.

FIG. 93. Orange Scallop Shells.

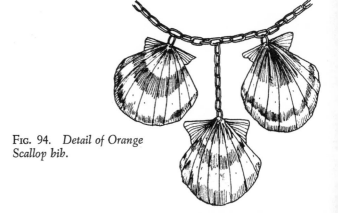

FIG. 94. Detail of Orange Scallop bib.

Fig. 96. *All the components from a beachcombing expedition put together in a necklace.*

You will also want to have hemp rope, thread, large ring catch, jump rings and epoxy cement.

Steps

1. Clean and prepare shells, if necessary.

2. When you have all your materials gathered around you, measure the length of rope needed by holding it around your neck. You may want to finish it off with a large ring catch and jump ring. In that case you'll need to allow enough rope to turn under at each end and sew down. If you do not want a catch, then allow sufficient length to fasten under the center shell with epoxy cement.

3. Straighten out the hemp on your working surface and start planning your pattern, putting your materials along its length.

4. Once planned, you will attach the shells using the techniques described in this chapter—glueing with epoxy or hanging by jump rings. Lash the feathers on with nylon thread, drilling holes where necessary. Imagine yourself sitting on the sand making a wild adornment for a tropical celebration.

A CLUSTER OF ARKS

Arks, in this case, are shells not ships. They are pure white, lightweight and deeply ribbed, and in this project they are hung in clusters one over the other along the front of a thin chain, with white beads separating the clusters and looking like fluted, clustered flowers.

Tools and Materials

A drill, wire cutter and pliers will do all.

Each cluster needs six Ark Shells, so that the number of shells depends on the length of your necklace and the number of clusters scattered along the chain. There are a number of arks—some very large and heavy—so pick the smallest, lightest in weight, and those with the deepest ribs. Suggested small and lightweight arks are: Transverse Ark

FIG. 97. *Pure white Ark Shell (Arca) of which there are several types and sizes.*

(*Arca transversa*), Chemnitz's Ark (*Arca chemnitzi*), Incongruous Ark (*Arca incongrua*), also one of the Pacific Shells, *Anadara* (*Tegillarca*) *nodifera*. Also check shell catalogs or a local shell shop. Fine chain, fine wire, white beads—mother of pearl, ivory, or a composition. The holes in the beads have to match the thickness of the chain, and the chain has to have links large enough to slip the wire through for attaching. Length of chain and wire and number of beads and shells all depend on the variables of sizes of shells, beads and length of necklace. Ring catch and jump rings.

Steps

1. Measure neck with cord and cut chain to match. For a long necklace, this measurement will be anywhere from 25 to 34 inches. You will want to leave between 5 and 6 inches on each side at the back without a shell decoration.

2. Clean shells, if necessary. If the Ark Shells are not white enough, bleach them. (See page 24.)

3. Put the chain flat on your working surface and mark the ending point at each side. Mark the center of the chain as well.

4. Make a temporary pattern of an overlapping double cluster of six shells—three on each side. Place the cluster over the chain, on its side with the open end facing the center. Add five or six beads, then a second double cluster with the open end facing the beads. Allow 2 or 3 inches of chain, then add another design of two clusters facing each other with the beads in between.

5. Move clusters and beads back and forth along the chain until you have a pleasing design.

6. Drill a hole in the top of each Ark Shell being used. (See page 40.)

7. Clusters are lashed together and then to the chain with fine wire in the following way. Fasten the wire to the chain at the spot where the points of the lowest two shells of a cluster will be fastened. Now clip off 15 inches of wire and fasten one end to a chain link. Thread the free end through the right-hand shell from bottom to top—inside to outside. Bring wire over to the left-hand shell and thread through from inside to outside. Fasten to the chain link nearest to the top points of the two shells. Then add the next right-hand shell, threading the wire through from bottom to top, then over to the left-hand shell, fasten to chain—and so repeat the process until the first cluster of six shells is attached to the chain. Bring wire end back through one of the holes on a top shell and clip off underneath.

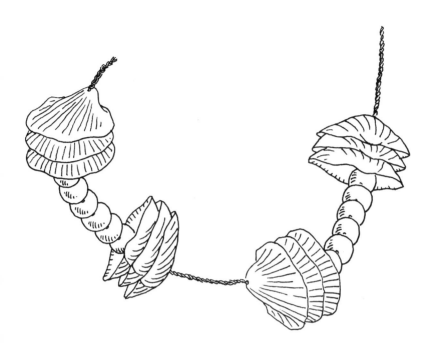

FIG. 98. *Arks, beads and chain combined into a necklace.*

8. Add beads, slipping them on the chain from the opposite end. Beads should disappear under the first two facing Ark Shells almost to the spot where the first wire joins the chain. Depending on the size of your ark and the size of your beads, this means about 1 to 1½ beads will be hidden.

9. Now add the second cluster of shells with the open end facing the beads and the open end of the first cluster. Follow the directions in Steps 6 and 7. If your second cluster does not come quite up to the spot you had planned, don't worry about it; the beads tend to slip a bit and you won't have any gaps between clusters.

10. When all the clusters and beads have been added, put on the catch and jump ring at each end of the chain.

DANGLING MUREX BRACELET

A chunky bracelet of heavy link chain and dangling Murex Shells is an eye catcher.

Tools and Materials

A drill and two pairs of pliers.

A link bracelet and oval jump rings. Ten to twenty 1-inch Murex Shells—the best are probably small specimens of Rose Murex (*Murex recurvirostris rubidus*) which are 1 inch long and are pink, orange, cream or red. Look for other murex varieties in white or tan, spiney or plain.

Steps

1. Clean and prepare shells, if necessary.

2. Stretch out the bracelet and plan how many Murex Shells you want to hang on it—one, two or three to a link.

3. Through the lower end of the canal on each shell, drill a hole large enough to hold a jump ring. (See page 40.)

4. Open the jump rings. Slip each one through a hole on a shell, then over a link of the bracelet. Close the jump rings.

Variation

You can use any of the Gastropods that are no more than 1 inch long, or a mixture of two or more varieties. In fact, almost all of the previously described necklace designs can be adapted to bracelets.

Fig. 99. *Assorted small Murex Shells.*

FIG. 100. *Two designs for a bracelet of hanging Murex Shells.*

BRASS-BOUND SNAIL PIN OR PENDANT

A flat brown Tree Snail from Puerto Rico is backed with an oval of gleaming brass for a magnificent pin.

Tools and Materials

Jeweler's saw, pliers, metal scriber, file, soldering iron or gun.

A large brown Tree Snail Shell, 2⅛ × 2½ inches. A piece of 18-gauge brass, 3¼ inches square. A bar pinback. Solder and flux, asbestos tile and rubbing alcohol. Crocus cloth, tracing paper, carbon paper and clear nail polish.

Steps

1. Make a tracing of the shell with the point of the opening at the top of your design.

2. Draw an oval around the tracing of the shell. Mine is 2⅞ inches wide and 3¼ inches long, but final measurements depend on the size of the shell.

3. Make a second line 3/16 of an inch *inside* the outline of the shell. This will form the shoulder of metal on which the shell will rest.

4. Now draw four inward facing triangles approximately ⅜ inch long along the shell outline. These will form the prongs to hold the shell in place.

5. Transfer the design to the metal using carbon paper. Remove tracing and carbon paper and retrace the black line with a metal scriber. Wash off all black with rubbing alcohol.

6. Cut out design with a jeweler's saw. (See page 42.)

7. Cut back on each side of the triangles to the shell outline mark. You may have to make these cuts just a bit deeper after you test the prongs on the shell.

8. Anneal the metal to make it easier to bend the prongs as the shell will not stand too much pressure. The metal will discolor, so go over it with crocus cloth. Also file all edges smooth, and angle the outside edge with the file to give a thicker look to the metal.

9. Clean the back of the metal with powdered kitchen cleanser to remove any grease before soldering on the pinback. The pinback will be positioned at the top one-quarter of the metal so it will not interfere with the prongs, and will keep the pin from falling forward when pinned to fabric. Solder on pinback. (See page 106.)

10. File off excess solder. Again polish with crocus cloth if there has been any discoloration from the soldering heat.

Fig. 101. *A large, dark brown Puerto Rican Tree Snail Shell.*

11. Pull up the prongs to an almost vertical position. Prongs should be pulled up slowly to allow the metal to adjust. An abrupt hard pull might snap the metal.

12. Since the shell is thick, the prongs will be almost at right angles to the flat oval base. Put the shell in position. Mark the approximate bend-over line with the scriber and adjust cut at the base of the prongs. Take out the shell and start the bend with the pliers. Put the shell back in its final position and very carefully finish the bending, working on opposite prongs.

13. File off any plier marks and polish with crocus cloth. Cover metal with clear nail polish to prevent tarnishing.

Variation

To turn the design into a pendant, drill two holes at the top of the metal oval about ½ to ¾ inches apart. Bend a 2¼-inch length of brass wire in half to form a pyramid, with the ends as far apart as the two holes on the pendant. Round each end of the wire, file smooth and bend up into hooks. Bring the hooks through the holes, with the hook part facing outward. Open the jump ring, slip it over the middle point of the wire and onto a neck wire or chain and close the opening.

FIG. 102. Brass-bound Snail pin or pendant.

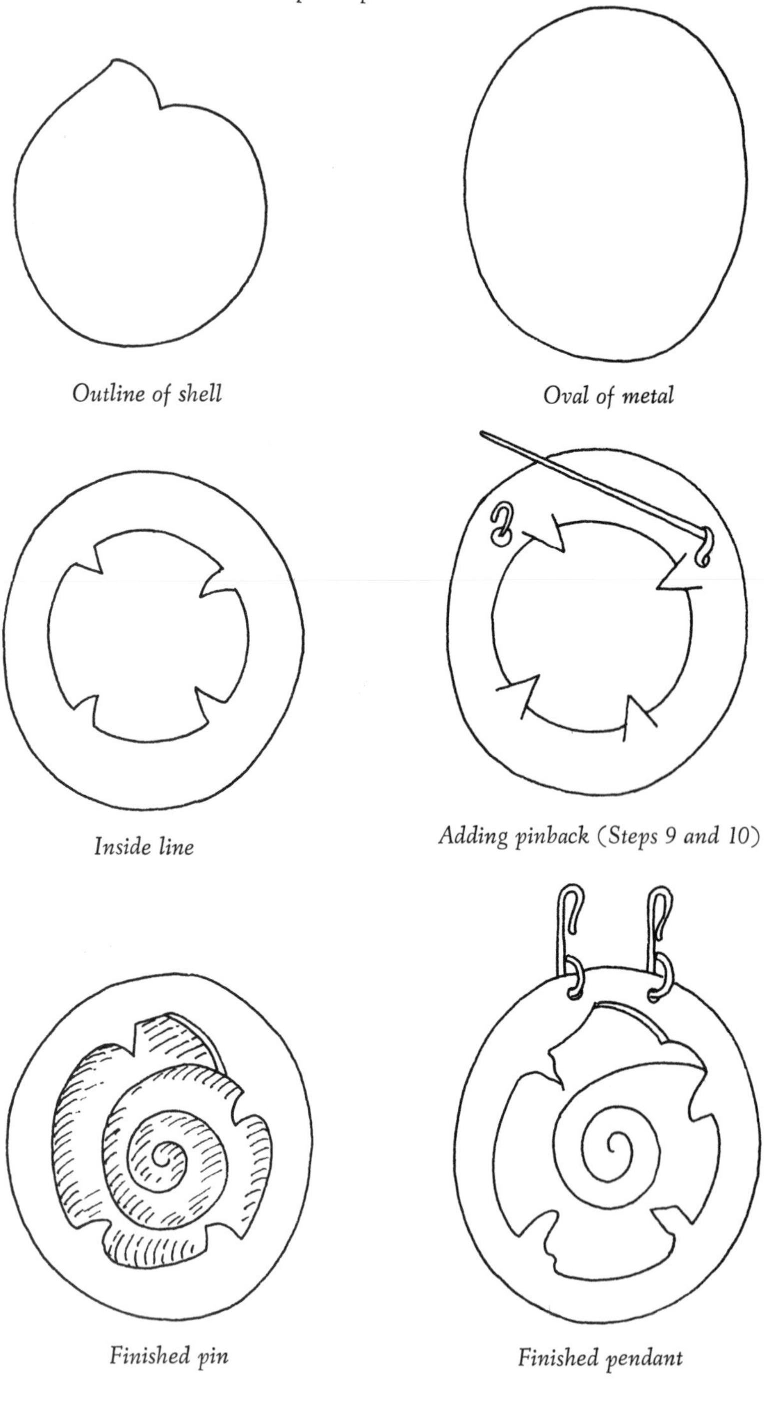

Outline of shell

Oval of metal

Inside line

Adding pinback (Steps 9 and 10)

Finished pin

Finished pendant

CAT'S EYE EARRINGS

Cat's Eye is the common name for the operculum of the snail type of shell. Each snail has one attached to its "foot," and it serves both to protect the foot and to act as the door of the shell, closing off the opening. The area against the foot has the soft shine of porcelain; the outside is duller and is often marked in a design of concentric rings. Some operculums are darkly colored in the center with a white edge—hence the name cat's eye. Others are oval with swirled markings. And all can be the basis of the simplest of all earrings to make.

Tools and Materials

The only tool needed is a toothpick for mixing and applying epoxy cement.

Otherwise you will need two operculums ½ to ⅝ inches across, earring backs with a flat or slightly concave metal disk in front, and epoxy cement.

Fig. 103. *Three Operculums, the lower two often called cat's eyes.*

153

Steps

1. This is a one-step operation. Mix epoxy cement and apply it to the metal disk of the earring backs and to the cat's eyes. Put the operculums in position and let dry for 24 hours. And that's all there is to it.

Variation

You can also use two pieces of button coral, matched for size. Or, attach button coral to a length of fine chain with epoxy cement, and link chain to earring back with a jump ring.

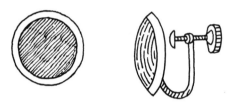

Fɪɢ. 104. *Cat's eye earrings.*

Fɪɢ. 105. *Earring designs using Button Coral.*

154

LIMPET EARRINGS

Limpet and Dove Shells in tans and white are combined to make dangling earrings with an oriental look.

Tools and Materials

Drill, pliers and metal file will take care of everything.

You will need 20 Limpets—and pick whatever genus is available, as there are a number all looking more or less alike to the untutored eye. The most practical suggestion is to find or buy those with a center hole as part of the original shell formation. In addition, add 12 Common Dove Shells (*Columbella mercatoria*) which are ½ to ¾ inches in length. Two earring backs with a ring in front and a concave disk above the ring. Approximately 16 inches of fine brass or silver wire, 22- or 25-gauge. Epoxy cement.

FIG. 106. *Two limpets plus finished earrings.*

Steps

1. Clean and prepare shells, if necessary. Drill a hole in ten Dove Shells, drilling from the inside of the canal out to the curved middle of the shell. Do not drill the other two Doves. If you have been lucky, your limpets all have holes; if not, drill all that need it. (See page 40.)

2. Curl over one end of the wire into a ⅛- to ³⁄₁₆-inch circle. Thread the free end through the outside of one limpet, through a Dove Shell, then from inside to outside of another limpet so that the Dove Shell is enclosed by two limpets. Curl the free end over into another circle and clip excess off. Repeat until you have ten clusters.

3. Hook two clusters together vertically by opening up one circle and slipping it over the circle of another cluster. Repeat with three more clusters, so that you have one 3-cluster string and one 2-cluster string for one earring. Repeat process for other earring.

4. Slightly open the top circle on each cluster. Hook a 3-cluster and a 2-cluster string over the ring on the front of the earring finding. Close each circle. Repeat for other earring.

5. Prop up the earrings so that the flat disk is in a horizontal position. Mix epoxy cement and put a drop on each metal disk. Press an undrilled Dove Shell into each disk horizontally with the channel facing downward toward the cluster of shells. Let dry for 24 hours.

Variations

You can use beads in place of Dove Shells, particularly if you do not have a drill. The limpet clusters can also be used as necklace pendants. Several clusters can be strung along a chain as a short bib necklace, or you can have clusters on a long chain.

HANGING CONE EARRINGS

Cone Shells are ideal for these earrings with two cones combined with wire to form delicate, baroque-style ornaments.

Tools and Materials

Drill, pliers, hammer and a metal file are your tools.

Four Cone Shells (*Conus*) no longer than 1⅜ inches. Approximately 12 inches of brass or silver wire, 22-gauge. This measurement depends on how long and how wide the hanging support will be. Carpet thread and white paper. Block of wood and fine nails or brads. Two earring

Fig. 107. *Three sizes of cones.*

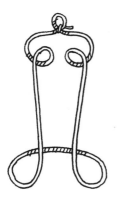

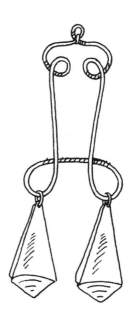

Fig. 108. *Wire and cone earrings.*

157

backs with small wire loops in front. Six jump rings, crocus cloth and clear nail polish.

Steps

1. Clean and prepare shells, if necessary.

2. Place two Cone Shells side by side on a piece of paper with ¼-inch space between the widest parts and the narrow point of the opening facing up. Trace around the shells, then remove them from the paper. Loop a length of carpet thread on the paper, following the design of the drawing on this page. Lightly trace the outline of the thread, then remove the thread and measure so that you will know the amount of wire needed for each earring.

3. Place the paper pattern over a block of wood, and lightly hammer brads or small nails through the paper into the wood, following the traced pattern.

4. Now, starting at the top, curve the wire around the brads, following the loops and straightaways of the tracing. Make two wire forms.

5. Using pliers twist the wire at the top to form a loop.

6. Drill a hole at pointed end of channel of each shell. (See page 40.)

7. Open the four jump rings and insert each ring through the hole in a shell, then into a bottom loop of a wire form. Close jump rings.

8. Attach each twisted wire loop to an earring back loop with a jump ring.

9. Polish the wire with file and crocus cloth to remove any nicks or scratches. Cover wire with clear nail polish to prevent tarnishing.

Variation

Use Murex Shells or Olive Shells in the same design.

PART II

SHELLS
MOLDED
AND
MODELED

5

How to Encase Shells in Resin

COMBINING the classic shapes of shells with modern plastic leads to some beautiful designs that are useful and decorative and which preserve the shells in all their beauty. There are two basic techniques: one is pouring a liquid, transparent casting resin into molds to be air dried; the second one consists of melting small plastic crystals, clear or colored, in a form in a kitchen oven.

This chapter will describe these processes in detail, as well as give you basic designs from which you can develop many variations.

TOOLS

The tools needed are minimum in number and very simple. *Wooden stirrers* to mix the casting resin and hardener. Small one-ounce or larger *mixing cups,* depending on the size of your project—these can be either paper or plastic throwaway types. A plastic *measuring cup* with measurements marked in ounces. An *eyedropper. Tweezers* for placing shells in the molds—the craft type with long, pointed ends are best. These are usually sold as jewelry-making or soldering tweezers. Long *pins* for pricking out bubbles. A *carpenter's level* for checking working surface. *Metal bookends* as supports for some projects.

MATERIALS

There are a number of products on the market under various trade names, but all have the two basic components: *a clear plastic pouring resin* and a *hardener* or *catalyst.* In addition, some manufacturers make a *surface hardener* which is added to the last layer of the casting. Plastic *cleaner* for your tools and *thinner* are also available. *Mylar sheet* on which to turn out your mold. *Pigments,* either opaque or transparent, for coloring the resin. A paste or liquid *mold-release* will be needed. *Silicone adhesive* is used to attach pieces of cast plastic to each other. One product has a *promoter* which speeds up the thickening time of the resin liquid—especially helpful when you are adding shells to a mold.

Plastic *baking* or *cooking crystals* are sold in clear granules as well as in 18 assorted colors. Some manufacturers supply only the clear crystals, but these can be colored with powdered tempera colors.

Shells, sand, pieces of seaweed, dried sea horses, starfish, all can be used as surface decorations or suspended in the plastic.

Molds to fit your projects—plastic or glass for the poured resin, and metal for the baking crystals. *Chains* and *jewelry findings,* and *hangers*

FIG. 109. *Liquid casting resin tools, left to right: carpenter's level, eyedropper, small container, long pin, stirrer, angled tweezer. In back is a metal bookend.*

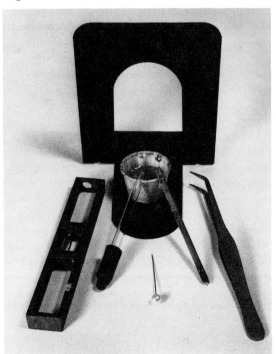

for wall plaques. Protective adhesive *felt* for the bottom of some objects. Plain or wet-and-dry *sandpaper* or powdered *pumice* for polishing some surfaces.

HOW TO MIX LIQUID CASTING RESIN

There are a number of products on the market under different trade names, but each one will have the identifying phrase of liquid casting (or pouring) plastic or resin. Also, with every product you get a hardener or catalyst to stiffen the basic liquid into a hard, glass-like casting. This action is very similar to that of epoxy cement which only becomes hard when the two liquids are mixed together.

Each product has a different proportion of hardener to liquid plastic, so follow the directions given by the manufacturer. Be careful when stirring in the hardener that you do not stir too hard and create air bubbles. If you do, let the bubbles rise to the surface and prick them out with a pin.

Only mix enough plastic to fill part of the mold. There are several reasons for this—each one as important as the other. The drying plastic creates a great deal of heat which would warp a plastic mold. The liquid plastic also might be prevented from drying evenly if you have a large quantity in your mold. If you are embedding shells or other objects in the plastic, you will need to add them on hardened material at different levels. If the mold is completely filled with plastic, the shells will sink to the bottom, never to rise again. Also, by pouring successive layers, you can change the color of your plastic at different levels, creating exciting designs.

Word of Warning. The setting times listed by manufacturers are for optimum conditions. You will find there are variations depending on weather, temperature and humidity.

ADDING COLOR

If you are embedding shells in plastic, the clear transparent material is most effective. However, you may want a thin base of color, or your design may use shells on the surface of a plastic shape with a contrasting color background.

Colors are available as pigments in tubes; some are opaque, and others only become opaque if used in quantity. Then there are transparent resin dyes which are truly transparent and are available in many colors and shades.

The pigments and dyes are added before the hardener, and it is best to add only a little color at a time until the proper shade is achieved. For instance, a medium shade is obtained by adding only four drops of dye to one ounce of liquid plastic. So add, drop by drop, from an eyedropper, stirring gently with a wooden coffee stirrer to mix the color into the plastic without creating air bubbles—a tricky process! Add pigments slowly from their squeeze tubes, again stirring carefully.

Once you have the right color, add the hardener in proportion to the resin, remembering also to add enough for the drops of color. Average proportions are four or five drops of hardener to an ounce of liquid resin, but in all cases be guided by the manufacturer's directions. Too much hardener will create too much heat during the drying process, too little and the liquid takes too long to dry; in either case the mold will be damaged. Don't be upset if you spoil a piece in the learning process—it happens to everyone.

Word of Warning. Since you will be pouring at least three layers to fill your mold, make a record of the amount of pigment added to the liquid resin, so that you can repeat this formula for each layer and end up with a fairly even color casting. Also, if you are planning on each layer being lighter or darker, you will know how much to increase or decrease the color.

TYPES OF MOLDS

You will find molds on display wherever you buy liquid casting resin. These molds are of three types. One is a thin but stiff plastic which can be re-used many times. These are for open castings in which the final top surface of pouring is a flat one. The second is a flexible plastic mold called "3-D" that forms a full round object—a figure, an animal and many other designs. This is peeled off after the casting has set and can be re-used. However, most of the designs are not applicable for this book. The third type is also a full round, but is made of thin glass which is broken after the plastic has hardened. The shapes are usually of all kinds of fruit; you can also get round balls of several sizes.

You will find a wide selection of molds in the catalogs of many mail order houses, particularly American Handicrafts and Specialty Products whose addresses are listed in the back of this book.

A fourth mold is one you make yourself from plaster of Paris. The process is fully described in Chapter 6. The plaster of Paris mold is covered with a coat of lacquer, shellac or varnish. When thoroughly dry

Fig. 110. *Three shapes of plastic molds.*

and just before casting, the surface is rubbed with paste mold-release which assures a clean release of your casting from the mold.

You can also use various glass or ceramic containers that you have around the house, again rubbing the inside with the paste mold-release.

Each project will specify a particular type and size of mold, based on available commercial molds. But you can vary the projects by using other sizes that you have found and which fit the design.

PREPARING MOLDS

A stiff plastic mold needs no preparation. It is flexible enough so that a release coating is not necessary. Just make sure that it is clean and dry, that is, there is no grease or dust on the inside surface.

Expendable glass molds just need to be dust free, as after the liquid plastic hardens the mold is broken away from the casting. You can also use a worn-out electric light bulb from which the metal end and filaments have been removed.

A heavier glass or ceramic mold that is not broken away from the plastic casting will need a release coating. One type is a wax-like paste which is applied over the surface with a clean cloth. The other is a liquid silicone which is wiped on with a tissue and the excess wiped off with a second tissue. These molds can be glass dishes, custard cups, decorative pudding molds, or rectangular or square glass ice-box storage containers.

165

FILLING MOLDS

Your working surface *has to be level,* and you will have to check this with a carpenter's level. If your table slants and it is impossible to make it level, then wedge small pieces of cardboard under your mold until an even surface is achieved. Unless you are careful about this, your casting will be uneven in thickness, and since the top surface of your casting is often the bottom of a finished piece, the bottom will be on a slant.

Since flexible molds, glass molds and pyramid and half-round stiff plastic molds do not have a base, they all need a special support to keep them in position during pouring and hardening. Cut a hole in the bottom of a cardboard carton that is deep enough for the length of the mold. Make the hole large enough for the widest part of a flexible or stiff plastic mold to slip through, but not wider than the supporting flange. The mold will hang free from this supporting flange. The hole for a round glass mold is cut just slightly smaller than the widest part and the mold is braced in position by pressure.

Before you measure and mix casting resin and hardener, check the quantity of liquid needed for your mold by filling the mold with cold water and then pouring the liquid into a plastic measuring cup. If you are going to fill the mold at one pouring, then this will be the quantity you will mix. But in most cases two or three pourings are best, so you will be dividing this quantity. Work out the proportion of liquid plastic to hardener according to the manufacturer's directions. If you are adding color, also add this to your formula. Make written notes of measurements so that if you have to make a second casting of that mold you will have your records handy.

If you are embedding shells in the plastic and are therefore pouring the liquid in layers, pour water from the measuring cup back into the mold to the depth you will cover with your first layer—approximately ¼ inch. Check cup measurement and record the amount in *ounces.* When you are pouring in layers, you will be mixing only enough material for each layer. You must also keep a record of the amount of color you use. You will be able to judge by the quantity of liquid for the first layer just how much to mix for the second, third and perhaps even a fourth layer. Your embedments will take up space, so you will end up with liquid left over which is all to the good—better some left over than not enough.

Wipe out the mold with tissues until it is dry and then let it stand to become thoroughly dry, as any water will spoil your casting.

Measure out the right quantities of resin and hardener stirring them carefully together for half a minute until they are well mixed. Pour into

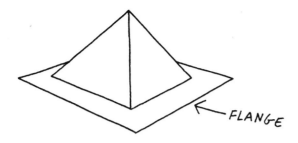

FLANGE

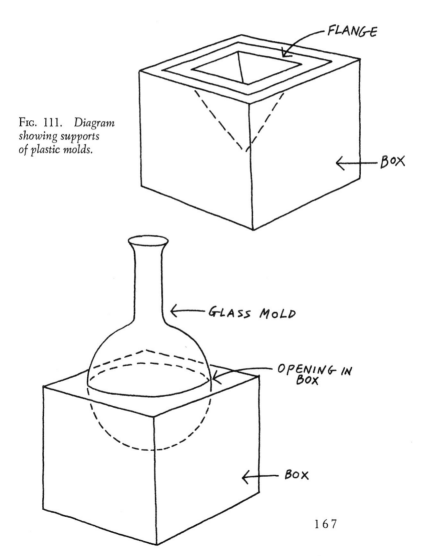

FLANGE

Fig. 111. Diagram showing supports of plastic molds.

BOX

GLASS MOLD

OPENING IN BOX

BOX

the mold, along the surface of a pouring stick—a wooden coffee stirrer—to minimize the chances of bubbles. When the surface is tacky, add your embedments. Mix next layer and pour it in. The gelling or stiffening time depends on the manufacturer's directions. In this stage you will also have to use your own judgment, and you will become more experienced with each project.

If you are adding several shells at different levels, you may find yourself mixing only small quantities of material for very shallow layers. In some cases you may not be completely covering a shell because the next shell may be overlapping this layer. However, start with a simple design of embedding only one shell until you are used to the process.

Word of Warning. Some materials are based on a formula of reducing the amount of hardener for successive pourings, so check the manufacturer's directions.

PREPARING EMBEDMENTS

All material to be embedded has to be free of dust, loose particles or any oil—even oil from one's own fingers. After cleaning, be sure that no water remains on or inside the shells. You will have to be particularly careful of the Snail Shells as water will lurk in the point forever, or so it will seem.

One of the problems of casting is the presence of air bubbles. This is especially true if you are casting the Snail Shells—murex, fig, Scotch bonnet, cone, olive—to name only a few. All shells with cavities have to be filled with liquid resin *first* before embedding in your mold. Mix a small amount of resin, making a guess as to the quantity needed to fill half the shell cavity. Pour in carefully. If you have a large opening, use a small funnel, or construct one of aluminum foil made into a cornucopia with an opening at the point. After the first layer is in, tap the shell lightly on your working surface to settle the liquid. You will also find that turning the shell, with the point held downward, will help in filling the whole interior and releasing any air. Let dry in a braced, level position—point down. When cool and dry, add the final layer of plastic resin to the inside of the shell. You can test for dryness by leaving a little resin in a mixing cup. Let second and final layer dry, then proceed with the embedding process.

REMOVING CASTING FROM MOLD

The casting has to harden before it is removed from the mold, but it should still be warm as then the stiff mold will be more pliable, and it will be easier to spread the sides a bit to pop out your casting. Press the mold back into shape so it can be re-used.

The average hardening time is two to three hours (this can be longer) so test the top surface with your wooden mixing stick to see how hard it is. If the top is only a bit sticky, unmold your casting onto a mylar-covered surface as the resin will not stick to this material, and the casting, exposed to the air, will dry much faster.

The stretchable 3-D plastic mold has to be removed when the casting is set but still warm as the mold will then stretch and pull away easily. Rub the outside of the mold with slightly wet soap before removing. Do *not* use detergent as that will cause the mold to stick to itself as you roll it off. The mold will return to its original shape. Do not handle casting until it has been well dried right side up on the mylar sheet.

Since the heavier glass or ceramic re-useable molds have been wiped with a mold-release, there should be no trouble turning out your casting for its final hardening.

Expendable glass molds will be broken away from the casting, so they are a one-time-use affair. Be very careful, though, in breaking the glass. Slip the mold inside a paper bag. Then, holding the top of the bag firmly in your grasp around the glass pouring neck, tap lightly against a hard surface until the glass shatters. Reach inside the bag with a gloved hand and remove the casting. All this has to be done carefully as you do not want to nick the surface of the casting nor cut your fingers on the broken glass. Let casting harden on a mylar sheet.

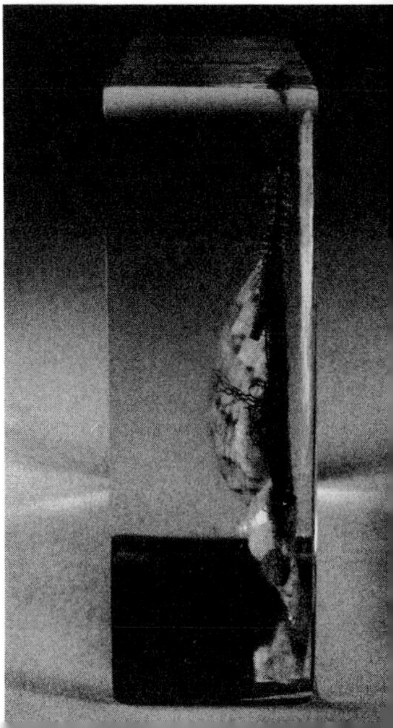

FIG. 112. *Side view of rectangular casting showing depth of shells in the casting.*

FINAL POLISHING OF SURFACE

Most clear resin castings will be unscratched and smooth, but once in a while one will need polishing. There are many methods—some involving electric buffing machines—but here are the simplest ones.

If you have deep scratches or an uneven surface, go over an area a little larger than the damaged part with wet-and-dry sandpaper attached to a small wooden block. Move the block around with a circular motion. The sandpaper is made in several grades; start with the coarsest grit and work down to the finest, using plenty of water and washing off the surface well before using the next finer grit. Once the scratches are out, the next step is the final polish.

You can use a fine polishing compound on a soft cloth—a Simoniz cleaner for instance—and finish up with an auto wax. There are also kits that contain polishing and scratch removal materials.

Many craft stores sell liquid glaze coats or spray coatings that add a thin, final coat to cover any surface blemishes. Personally, I do not like spray-can materials as these are harmful and should not be used indoors in an unventilated room.

CEMENTING SEPARATE CASTINGS TOGETHER

Most liquid casting resin shapes are held together with a silicone adhesive which is formulated especially for assembling separate plastic units. It is applied by eyedropper or small brush, relying on capillary action to carry the liquid across the joining area. Sometimes a hypodermic needle is used but this equipment is hard to come by.

The first step in joining two surfaces is to make sure that they fit closely together without forcing. However, very slight differences can be overcome by the silicone adhesive as it softens the surfaces to be attached and levels out both edges. If you have a very bad bump, go over it with wet-and-dry sandpaper and water as described in the previous section.

Also, before adding the adhesive you will have to work out a method of bracing two pieces so that they are held in an unmoving position for about 30 minutes or until the bond is hard and dry. You can brace the upright piece against a wooden box, a wall or metal bookends. Sometimes a small bag filled with metal shot can be placed on top of the upright piece as a pressure weight, but you have to be very careful of the balance as it could slip during the drying period and break the seal.

In the case of thin rectangles or squares (tiles) being fitted together to make a container, place the narrow edge of one "tile" along the top edge of the bottom tile in a right-angle position to form one side of the container. Tip the top tile back just slightly, and flow the silicone liquid under the full length of the joint with either an eyedropper or brush. Carefully bring the top tile back into position but do not press down for at least half a minute. The silicone will act on both facing surfaces, melting them a bit and so forming an even surface. After this wait, you can press down a bit to squeeze out any air bubbles, but do not rock or move the two tiles or press out any of the silicone. The first five minutes of hardening are very crucial, *so do not disturb the two tiles during this time.*

Then, after a 30-minute drying period you can add a "ribbon" of silicone on the inside of the joint as an extra seal. Let dry for 30 or more minutes. Then add the next upright tile, following the same procedures, until all four sides of your container are attached to the bottom tile.

Baking crystal projects can be assembled with epoxy cement. Epoxy cement can also be used to join baking crystal forms to commercial plastic boxes.

BAKING OR COOKING CRYSTALS

This material, as its name implies, is a *heat-treated plastic* and is very easy to handle. It is sold in ⅛- to ¼-inch-long cylindrical cuts of mostly transparent plastic. The crystals are poured into a *metal mold*, ranging from straight-sided *container covers* to small metal *cookie cutters, muffin tins,* small *pie plates* or metal *pudding molds.* Usually the depth of the crystals in a mold is ⅛ to ¼ inch.

Fig. 113. *Packets of plastic crystals and an opened envelope showing shape of individual crystals. These are in many colors.*

When the molds are filled with either a single color or several to give a mottled appearance—such as brown, orange and a bit of green for a tortoise-shell effect (the colors will not run into each other), they are then put into a preheated 375° to 400° kitchen oven. The baking time is 30 minutes or until the crystals have melted to a smooth surface. If you bake them less than this, the surface will still be rough-rubbly. The timing is not exact and you will have to work by trial and error. Several small molds are placed on a *cookie sheet* for stability. If the cookie cutters are open at the bottom, place a sheet of aluminum foil over the surface of the cookie sheet.

Several effects can be achieved with the combination of shells and melted crystals, and these will be developed in the project section. It is enough to say as general directions that shells can be placed in a design at the bottom of a mold and the crystals poured over them. Or, the mold can be half filled with crystals melted partway to a rubbly surface, a shell placed in position, the mold filled to the top and the regular melting process followed. This method will bury your shell between two layers of plastic. Or, crystals are poured into the mold part way, shell added, then more crystals, and baked. The mold can be almost filled to the top, melted to a rubbly surface, the shell or shells put on top and a few crystals placed around the shell edges. Put back in the oven until a shiny surface results. The melted plastic will hold the shell in position, but the shell will be a surface decoration and not covered by plastic.

When the mold is cool the plastic material will shrink away from the sides and can be turned out.

You can also make special and individual shapes by folding aluminum foil into a container and placing it on a baking sheet before filling with the crystals.

Holes for hanging pendants or the components for mobiles are made in the plastic with either a drill or a hot ice pick, thin nail or metal skewer.

On the following pages individual projects will be described step by step. Each one is a basic approach, and with this knowledge and acquired skill you can then develop other designs. So happy cooking and casting.

WHITE SCALLOP NAPKIN HOLDER

This is a very simple but effective design and the best one to try as a first resin-pouring project. The base is a rectangular mold, and set upright in this base are two large white Scallop Shells, facing each other with space between to place a pack of napkins.

Tools and Materials

Measuring cup, disposable mixing cups, wooden coffee stirrers and eyedropper.

Clear liquid pouring resin, hardener, transparent color (optional), two white Scallop Shells 4½ x 5 inches. These are the shells one buys in houseware departments as Coquille St. Jacques baking shells. Rectangular plastic mold 3 x 6 inches and 1¹⁄₁₆ inches deep. Sheet of mylar and two metal bookends.

Steps

1. Measure out the resin for the first ¼-inch layer; add color if you wish. Measure and mix in hardener. Pour first layer and let it harden.

2. Mix and pour a ⅜-inch second layer. This should bring the resin up to the ⅝-inch mark on your mold.

3. When the plastic is almost jelled, slip a metal bookend under each long side of the mold, as these will support the two shells in position as the plastic resin hardens. Now insert the shells in the top layer with the flat hinge back down. Place them ⅜ inch in from each long side and at the halfway mark of each long side, convex sides facing outward.

4. Move the bookends close enough to support the curved side of the shell in an upright position. Shells should be upright, not curved toward each other, and the bottom of each curved side should stick out over the side base line.

5. Let the casting harden. Then add the third layer which should bury the bottom ⅜ inch of the shell in plastic. Top surface of resin will be ¹⁄₁₆ inch below top edge of mold. Let harden.

6. Now check the top surface. If it is irregular or has shrunk too low, float on a thin layer of the resin mixture. Even if you have used a color in the other layers, this thin coat can be clear as the color will show through.

7. Remove casting from the mold while it is still warm and the top layer is almost hard—its surface might be just a bit tacky. Let dry on a mylar sheet. Continue to support the shells with the bookends until the base is crystal hard so that there is no chance of bumping them and breaking the bond.

Variations

Use Clam Shells, large Oyster Shells, Lion's Paw (*Pecten nodosus*) or small Sea Pens instead of the Scallop Shells. Also, the first pouring can be a dark color and the rest of the casting clear transparent resin.

Fig. 114. *Lion's Paw Scallop* (Pecten nodosus), *which is suggested in* "Variations." *The White Scallop is shown in Fig. 36.*

Fig. 115. *Two views of scallop napkin holder (page 172).*

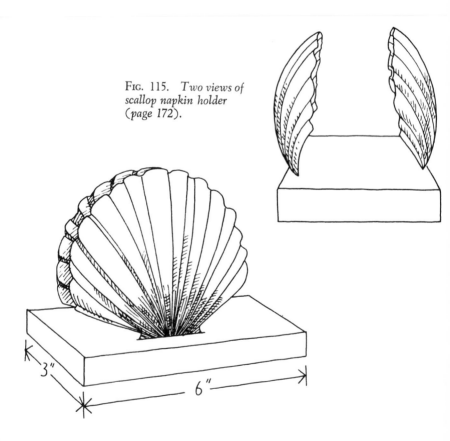

3"

6"

STARFISH NAPKIN HOLDER

A clear and sparkling design is made from a cast rectangular base and two disks each with a Starfish (*Asterias* or others) or Sea Horse (*Hippocampus*) embedded in the plastic. This is a perfect holder for small party napkins.

Tools and Materials

Measuring cup, disposable mixing cups, wooden coffee stirrers, eyedropper, long pin and felt marker are all the standard tools for casting.

Three molds: a rectangular one 3 x 6 inches and 1$\frac{1}{16}$ inches deep, and two disks 2⅜ inches in diameter and 1 inch deep. Liquid pouring resin plus hardener. Two small starfish approximately 1¾ inches in diameter, or two sea horses, or two small sand dollars. A sheet of mylar and a pair of metal bookends (see Fig. 109).

Steps

1. Clean shells, if necessary.
2. Cast the disks first as these will have to be crystal hard when placed upright on the rectangular base. As you will not be using the full depth of these molds—only ⅝ of an inch—make three marks on the outside of the molds, using a black felt-tipped marker. Marks should be at ¼, ⅛, ¼ inch, measuring up from the bottom. These will show through the translucent molds and be your guide in pouring to the final ⅝-inch depth.
3. Mix liquid resin and hardener and pour a ¼-inch layer in each mold. Let dry.
4. When the surface in each is still sticky but thick enough to support the starfish, center it on the plastic, *top side facing downward*. (In this casting, as with many others, the bottom of the mold is really the outer face of your design as it will be the smoothest surface.)
5. Pour a very thin layer—⅛ inch—into each mold. Brace your starfish with the point of a long pin so that it will stay in position during the pouring. With either the mixing stick or the pin, break any bubbles or work them to the outer edge where they will break. This thin layer also cuts down on the heat which might damage a soft object like a starfish.
6. When this layer of resin has hardened, mix enough liquid for the final ¼-inch layer and pour into each mold. Fill to the top mark.
7. After the casting is hard on top but the mold is still warm, turn out on the mylar sheet and let dry until crystal hard.
8. Once the disks are hard, pour the bottom rectangle in three layers: ¼ inch, ⅜ inch, ⅜ inch. The top layer of resin should be jelled but not

hardened when you place the two disks upright, centered at the edge. The bottom of the disks will be immersed in this last layer. Support the two disks with bookends until the plastic has hardened. (See "White Scallop Napkin Holder," Steps 3 and 4, page 173.) Top layer of resin will be within $\frac{1}{16}$ inch of the top edge of the mold, allowing for a final thin layer of resin to smooth the surface.

9. Remove napkin holder from mold when firm but still warm and let harden thoroughly before using.

Variations

Substitute two sand dollars or sea horses for the starfish. In these two cases, mix a small quantity of resin and hardener and soak the sand dollars or sea horses in the liquid, then hang up by a piece of thread to dry. This will dry out any air remaining in the objects. If using small Calico Scallop Shells, place shell with convex side down into a fresh layer of plastic ($\frac{1}{8}$ inch thick) so that bubbles will not form around it. Next layer will come up over the edge and fill the shell hollow. Then the final layer after this, so that you are pouring four layers.

Instead of a round disk, use a 4-inch octagon-shaped mold. Place two sea horses facing each other in each mold.

Add color to the last pouring to make a contrasting background for your center design.

CIRCLE-IN-A-SQUARE NAPKIN RING

Clear plastic napkin rings add a modern look to a dining table and the floating shells are an individual touch.

Tools and Materials

Measuring cup, disposable mixing cups, wooden coffee stirrers, eye-dropper, felt marker, toothpicks and long pin.

You will be buying re-usable plastic molds, 3 x 3 inches and $1\frac{1}{16}$ inches deep. Depending on how many rings you are planning to make, you may want to buy two or three molds so that more than one ring can be made at a time. Small, straight-sided fruit-juice glasses, no more than 2 inches in diameter. Shells: small Gastropods which will be scattered at random as a center layer—turbonillas, coffee beans, cowries, wenteltraps, screwshells, loras, murex, doves, little whelks, Tampa drills, periwinkles, top shells, horns, zebras and many other small ones. Clear pouring resin plus hardener. Paste mold-release and a sheet of mylar.

FIG. 116. *Starfish.*

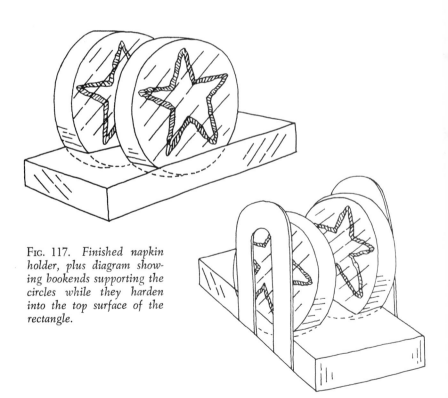

FIG. 117. *Finished napkin holder, plus diagram showing bookends supporting the circles while they harden into the top surface of the rectangle.*

Steps

1. Clean shells, if necessary.

2. Whether you use the top or bottom of the fruit-juice or other glass as your inner wall depends on which end has a straight side for at least 1¼ inches. Whichever end of the glass you use, cover the outside with a paste mold-release. Put the glass in the exact center of your rectangular mold. Put a very narrow line of paste around the bottom edge so that the liquid resin will not run under it. Repeat for the rest of the molds you are using.

3. Mix enough liquid resin and hardener to cover the bottom of the molds a little more than ⅜-inch deep. Pour in carefully, pressing down on the center glass. You may want to put a small weight on the top of each glass to make sure the pressure is kept up.

4. Add an extra teaspoon of plastic to what is left in your mixing container, plus the necessary hardener. Drop liquid from a toothpick into the opening of each shell to drive out the air and seal the area so that no bubbles will form in your casting. Let shells dry with the openings facing up.

5. When the plastic in the mold is partially hard and the top surface tacky but strong enough to support the shells, add your decorations with the shell openings facing both ways so neither side of the ring is a front side.

6. Pour in a ¼-inch layer of resin. If any shells move out of position, put them back in place with the long pin. Let dry.

7. Now pour the final layer and let harden. The top of this layer will be ⅟₁₆ inch below the top edge of the mold. Remove each mold from the casting when the top is hard or even when it is slightly tacky. But do not wait until the resin has cooled.

8. Let your casting dry on the mylar sheet until solid.

9. Repeat the process until you have completed the number of rings you need.

Variation

You can try putting the shells in a two-layer design. Half of the shells added on top of the first pouring, making that one only ¼ inch, then ¼ inch of resin, more shells when that is dry, ¼ inch to cover second lot of shells, and then the final pouring—making four pourings in all—and two layers of shells floating in space.

FIG. 118.   *Assorted small shells.*

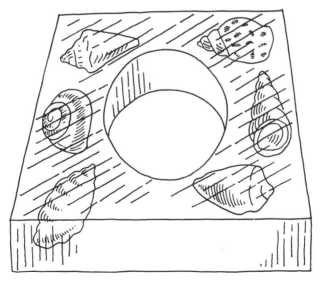

FIG. 119.   *Finished napkin ring.*

UNDERWATER PAPERWEIGHT

Make an imaginary scene in a square or half-round mold, using shells, beach sand and fine seaweed to bring back the feeling of hot summer days.

Tools and Materials

Measuring cup, disposable mixing cups, wooden coffee stirrers, eye-dropper, felt marker and long pin.

Liquid resin and hardener. Almost-square mold—2¾ x 3¾ inches and 1¹⁄₁₆ inches deep, or similar proportions. Approximately a teaspoon of coarse yellow sand. An assortment of small shells plus a 1⅜-inch Calico Scallop (*Pecten gibbus*), a small Starfish (*Asterias* or others) ¾ inch across, a ⅞-inch-long Sea Horse (*Hippocampus*) and a finely-cut bit of seaweed. (Beach-gathered shells should be cleaned.) Sheet of mylar.

Steps

1. Make sure shells are clean and dry. Wash sand and seaweed and let dry.

2. On a sheet of white paper draw the outline of your mold to exact size. Within this framework place your shells, starfish, sea horse, seaweed or whatever in their exact positions for the final design. Keep the sand separate but indicate with a pencil line the area it will occupy. The line of sand that indicates the bottom of your design is about ⅜ inch inside one lengthwise-edge margin.

3. Measure with water the amount of liquid plastic you will need to cover the mold to a ⅛-inch depth plus enough to fill the hollow in the Scallop Shell and any of the Snail Shell openings. Then mix resin and hardener and pour into the well-dried mold.

4. Fill the inside of the Scallop Shell, bracing it so the liquid will be level with the edge. Drop a little plastic into any Snail Shells.

5. When the surface of the resin in the mold is still a little sticky and the resin in the shell likewise, form the design. In this case you will be arranging the shells face up. Place a narrow oval of sand about ⅜ inch above what will be the bottom of your design, that is, the long side of the mold nearest to you as you work. The seaweed swoops up from this base to one side and will be partially under the Scallop Shell. Place the shell in the center and scatter the other small shells along the top of the sand, overlapping it a bit. Hook the tail of the sea horse in a piece of seaweed at the top right of the design.

6. Pour in about ¼ inch of clear resin and hardener. Pour over the

Fig. 120. *An underwater scene cast in clear pouring resin.*

Scallop Shell, letting the liquid flow over the design *very slowly*. You do not want any of your design, especially the sand, to float out of position. But having pressed everything into the sticky surface, you should be safe. Check for bubbles, and break any that form with the long pin.

7. When the surface is still tacky, add the starfish, leaning it at an angle against the scallop. Carefully pour in ¼ inch of clear resin and hardener. Let dry.

8. Pour another ¼ inch of resin and hardener, and let dry.

9. Now pour the final ⅛ inch up to the top of the mold, and let dry.

10. When the casting is almost cool, turn out on the mylar sheet and let dry.

11. If top surface is uneven or not clear, sand and polish. (Page 170.)

Variations

An assortment of various types of seaweed forming an overall pattern with or without a sand base.

A dome shape, 3 inches in diameter and 2 inches deep, can also be used for an underwater scene. Arrange the scene to conform to the shape of the mold.

Fig. 121. *Murex Shell*
(Murex florifer arenarius).

A SHIMMERING PYRAMID

The pyramid, a mysterious desert symbol, is cast here in clear resin with a shell captured and held inside. Use a murex which is also a Mediterranean shell from which the royal purple dye of the Roman emperors was made. A nice conceit for a pyramid paperweight.

Tools and Materials

Measuring cup, disposable mixing cups, wooden coffee stirrers, eye-dropper, felt marker, thread, and a thin nail 3 inches long.

Clear liquid resin and hardener, bright-green transparent dye, Murex Shell 1¼ inches long, a pyramid mold 2 x 2 x 2 inches, a sheet of mylar.

Steps

1. Clean shell and dry well.
2. Make a level support for the mold. (See page 166.)
3. Mix a small amount of resin and hardener and fill the point of the pyramid to a depth of ½ inch. At the same time fill the cavity of the shell with the mixed liquid.
4. When the resin inside the shell is no longer liquid, tie a piece of thread around the upper point of the shell. Hold the shell in the center

of the pyramid with the narrow bottom point just touching the top of the poured resin which should now be hardened to a tacky surface. Balance the nail across the top center of the pyramid and hold with pieces of sticky or masking tape. Wrap the free end of the thread around the center of the nail and fasten. This will suspend the shell in position.

5. Very carefully pour in ⅜ inch of clear plastic and let harden until the surface has begun to gel. Be sure that the shell is hanging directly in the center. Let dry.

6. Next mix and pour in ½-inch of resin. Repeat the hardening process. Remove thread and nail when your shell is held firmly in the plastic.

7. Mix and pour in another ½ inch of resin and let harden. These successive layers will prevent a build-up of heat.

8. The liquid is now almost to the top of the mold and the shell should be covered. You can either pour a last clear layer of resin so that your shell seems to float in clear water, or you can add a layer of bright green so that your shell seems to be balanced by its top point on the base of color. (See page 163.)

9. Let pyramid top harden, but remove mold before it is too cool and when the top is hard or slightly tacky.

10. Let the pyramid dry, broad side down on a sheet of mylar.

Variations

Use a Cone Shell in place of a murex. Or add small black-and-white Zebra Shells at different levels.

Insert a length of cord in the center of the last ¼ inch just after the plastic has been poured, to act as a hanger. The pyramid can be hung from the bottom of a decorative plant-hanger, on a wind chime, as part of a mobile, a Christmas tree decoration, or hung in a sunny window to turn and sparkle in the light. You can add it as the center knob of a plain, commercial lucite box, attaching it with silicone glue.

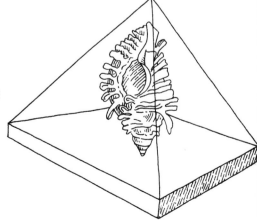

Fig. 122. *The Murex Shell held in clear plastic.*

TAKE YOUR PLACE

Cast small, thin rectangles of clear casting resin, embedding shells at one corner or across the top. These are re-useable place cards on which a guest's name is written with a white, easily-washed-off china-marking pencil. The supports are partially unbent paper clips.

Tools and Materials

Measuring cup, disposable mixing cups, wooden coffee stirrers, eye-dropper, black felt-tipped marker and long pin.

Your choice of small, rather flat shells. Liquid resin plus hardener. The mold is a plastic one, 2¼ x 2⅝ inches and 1⅛ inches deep—but you will not use all this depth. Large 2-inch paper clips. A sheet of mylar.

Steps

1. Clean shells and dry well.

2. As the molds are re-useable, you do not have to buy a mold for each place card. Plan on three or four pourings per mold. Decide, though, on how many you are going to make so that you will have enough shells available. Have a rough plan ready for the placement of the shells, either in one upper corner, both upper corners, or as a strip across the top—each one the same design or all totally different.

3. You will not be using the full depth of the mold, so mark the pouring measurements on the outside of the mold with a black felt-tipped pen. The mark will show through the translucent material. First

Fig. 123.   *Assorted small Scallop Shells.*

layer is ⅛ inch, next layer with shells is approximately ¼ inch, and the last layer ⅛ to ¼ inch, making the whole depth ½ to ⅝ inches. If any of the shells are snail-like, fill the openings with clear resin.

4. Mix enough clear resin and hardener to pour the first ⅛ inch in all your molds. Let harden until the surface is beginning to go from tacky to hard.

5. Add the shells according to your plan, *face downward,* as the bottom of the mold will be the front of the place card. Pour in the next layer of resin, covering the shells. Pour over a wooden stirrer so that the casting is bubble free and the shells are not disturbed. If any shells move out of position, push them back in place with a long pin.

6. When surface is almost hard, pour the next level and let dry until hardened but still warm. Turn out, face down, on a mylar sheet for the final drying.

7. Pour the rest of the place cards, following the above procedure.

8. When all are dry and hard, unfold large, 2-inch paper clips—two per card—leaving the outside loop in place. Turn back the rest of the clip to form an easel back and an outstretched balancing foot. (See Fig. 124.) As you are reversing the curve of the metal, do this bending slowly so as not to snap the clip.

Variation

If you have a favorite color for your table settings, color the clear resin to match or contrast.

Fig. 124. *Various designs for place cards, plus a diagram of the wire holder made from a paper clip.*

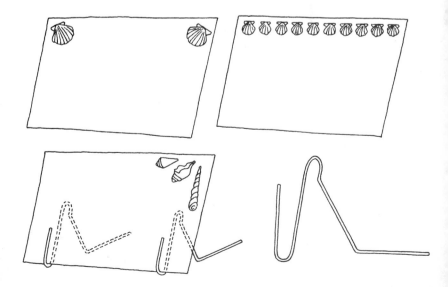

CRAZY DECORATION

Here is a fun way to mix the millenniums by using as a casting mold an electric light bulb with the filaments and metal end removed, then suspending a fossil shell in the clear casting resin. It becomes an outrageous pun on fossil fuel or light. The one shown in Fig. 125 is a left-hand fossil Cone (*Conus*).

Tools and Materials

Measuring cup, disposable mixing cups, wooden coffee stirrers, eyedropper, black felt-tipped marker, long pin, thread, and a thin nail 2 inches long.

The mold is a burned-out electric light bulb. The shell or shells can be regular present day ones, say a Nutmeg Shell (*Cancellaria reticulata*) or a small fossil shell if you are lucky enough to find one. In either case, the shell cannot be wider than the neck of the bulb. Liquid casting resin plus hardener. A sheet of mylar.

Steps

1. Remove the metal end and the filaments from a burned-out electric light bulb.

2. Decide on how many shells you are going to use for your design and just where they are going to be placed so that you can plan on the number of layers of resin you will be mixing and pouring. Clean shells and dry well.

3. Prepare the mold support. (See page 166.)

4. Mix enough casting resin for the ¼-inch first layer. Pour in and let harden.

5. If shell or shells are of the snail type, fill openings with resin so that they will not be releasing air bubbles once they are placed in the casting.

6. Drop in or suspend the fossil shell with string (see "A Shimmering Pyramid," Step 4, page 182). Add a ⅜-inch second layer of resin and let harden.

7. Continue mixing and pouring ⅜-inch layers until the shell is solidly supported, then remove the supporting string. Pour in the rest of the ⅜-inch layers until you reach the top. This pouring in layers keeps the resin from getting overheated.

8. Let everything harden until the glass feels slightly warm, then break the mold. (See page 169.) Let the casting dry on a sheet of mylar.

If you really want to fool the viewer, replace the metal light bulb end on the casting, holding it in place with epoxy cement.

You can also color the clear resin a soft shade as a dark color will hide the shell or shells.

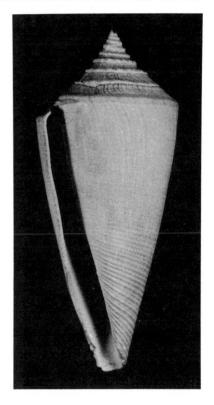

FIG. 125. *The left-hand fossil cone. At the present time, cones have an opening on the right side.*

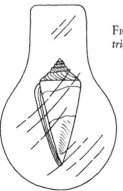

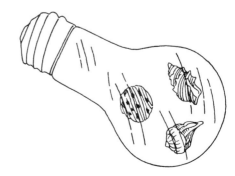

FIG. 126. *Cone embedded in an electric light bulb casting of liquid resin.*

STICK-ON CACHE-POT

Four-sided clear plastic cache-pots are made from five cast "tiles" each with shells encrusted in a center design, creating an airy and sparkling container.

Tools and Materials

Measuring cup, disposable mixing cups, wooden coffee stirrers, eye-dropper, a long pin.

Clear liquid resin plus hardener, two plaster of Paris tile-shaped molds, mold-release and shells. Make the design according to the shells you have or whatever is available at the local shell shop—but make a simple design that brings out the beauty of the individual shells. Silicon adhesive and epoxy cement. A sheet of mylar.

Steps

1. You will need five resin castings of flat ¾-inch-thick tiles. The shells will be added on top of the last layer of resin on four of the tiles that form the sides of the container. The other tile will form the bottom of the container.

2. Make a diagram of the placement of the clear resin tiles, so that you will have the right measurements for the bottom and sides of the container. Depending on the placement of the side and bottom "tiles" in the final construction, you have several options. Read on for a full explanation. Study the two layout diagrams for a container.

In Fig. 128a, the sides rest *on* the bottom tile which means you have a finished container 4 inches wide on each side, and 4¾ inches high.

In Fig. 128b, the bottom tile rests *inside* the four sides which makes a finished container 5½ inches wide on each side, and 4 inches high.

Following these two basic layouts you can develop your own size container, either square or oblong.

3. You will need to make two plaster of Paris molds of separate measurements. The molds are re-used for the resin castings.

Fig. 128a. One mold will be 4 x 4 inches, and ¾ inch thick. (Make three resin castings.)

One mold will be 4 x 2½ inches, and ¾ inch thick. (Make two resin castings.)

Fig. 128b. One mold will be 4 x 4 inches, and ¾ inch thick. (Make three resin castings.)

One mold will be 4 x 5½ inches, and ¾ inch thick. (Make two resin castings.)

4. Make the plaster of Paris molds for resin casting.

5. Look over your shells and lay out a pattern for each side. This can contrast or more or less match—all depending on how many shells you have of each variety. Four gray Scallop Shells (*Pecten*) with their hinged ends facing inward can be a very subtle design, or Dosina Shells with perhaps small Nassarius Shells in the middle: dog whelk, rattle or basket. Or, if you have some spectacular forms of Vase Shells (*Vasum muricatum*), or murex, or Spiny Chama (*Echinochama arcinella*), they can be used as a center of the design.

6. Mix and pour the several layers of resin in the two plaster of Paris molds until you have a tile ¾-inch thick. Before the last ¼-inch-deep pouring hardens, place your shells in the design you have laid out so that they are held along the edges or bottoms by the resin, but they must *not* be covered. Depending on the shells used, this means that your last layer may only be ⅛ inch deep.

7. Let the castings stiffen and before they cool completely, remove from the molds for the final hardening on a mylar sheet.

8. Repeat the pouring and shell design in the two molds again. Let stiffen and turn out on the mylar sheet to harden.

9. Make a fifth casting using the mold that is the size of the bottom of your container. This will be a plain tile without a shell decoration. Let harden and turn out on the mylar sheet.

10. Once all the castings have hardened, put them together with silicon adhesive. The bottom either supports the sides or slips into the space between the sides—whichever form you planned on.

Variations

You can color the clear liquid casting resin to contrast with the shells.

A solid color bottom with clear sides is very effective—or clear sides with a solid color top cover.

Pour a sixth tile—a plain one—as a cover for the open container, turning it into a box or even an ice tub if large enough. Add a large shell in the center as a lifting "knob."

Add madeleine pan forms of baking crystals (see "Crystal Madeleines" page 199) in place of shells, holding them in position on the sides of the container with epoxy cement or silicone adhesive after the tiles have hardened.

189

FIG. 127. *Several white Dosina Shells.*

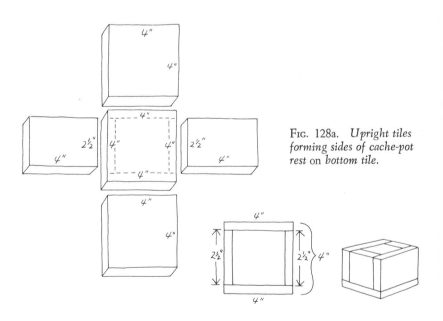

FIG. 128a. *Upright tiles forming sides of cache-pot rest on bottom tile.*

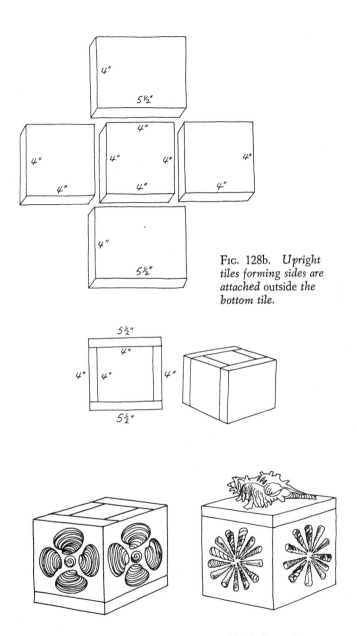

4"

5½"

4"

4"

4"

4"

4"

4"

4"

4"

4"

4"

5½"

FIG. 128b. *Upright tiles forming sides are attached outside the bottom tile.*

5½"

4"

4"

4"

4"

5½"

FIG. 128c. *Finished cache-pot and lidded container.*

SHELL STAND

The base is clear casting resin with the shell held above on a brass wire, giving the effect of water flowing under the shell.

Tools and Materials

Measuring cup, disposable mixing cups, wooden coffee stirrers, eye-dropper, black felt-tipped marker, long pin, pliers and crocus cloth.

A length of 16- or 18-gauge brass wire—straight wire, not spool wire. (Roughly measure the length needed with a piece of cord as the length and gauge depend on the size of the shell.) Large shell and, optionally, small shells. Liquid resin plus hardener and a plastic rectangular mold 3 x 5 inches, and 1¹⁄₁₆ inches deep. A sheet of mylar. Clear nail polish.

Two suggested shells are *Bursa rana,* an ivory and tan Snail Shell covered with whorls and spikes and very light in weight. The other is one of the family *Tridacnidae,* a clam type of shell in rose pink with white ruffles on each rib, looking like a fancy petticoat (see Fig. 129).

Steps

1. This non-soldered support is formed by bending a length of wire into cradling arms and a spread base. With the pliers bend one end of the wire into three 1-inch-long narrow loops, spread out like a bird's foot. This will be buried in the resin. Carry the wire upright as high as you want your shell to rest above the base—about 1¾ to 2 inches. Next, make three or four longer loops to act as supports for the shell, bending them up a bit to form a cradle or shallow saucer shape (see Fig. 130). The size of each top support will vary as it has to fit the shell to be displayed. File away any marks made by the pliers and polish with crocus cloth.

2. Mix and pour the first ¼-inch layer of clear casting resin. Let harden until just tacky. Pour a ¼-inch second layer. When this layer is tacky, pour the third ¼-inch layer. When this layer is beginning to thicken, plunge the lower end of the support into the center of the rectangle. Brace the wire in an upright position.

3. When the third layer is hard, pour in the final ¼-inch layer and let stand until the casting is just about hard but still warm. Take out of the mold and place on a sheet of mylar for final hardening.

4. Cover metal with clear nail polish so that it will not tarnish. Protect resin surface from any drops of nail polish.

5. Put shell over cradle.

Fig. 129. *A lacy,
clam-type shell*
(Tridacnidae) *from the
Pacific Ocean.*

Variations

Add color to the resin, either as a first layer with the rest clear or as a
solid color throughout.

Put a few small shells into the clear plastic, setting them in at different levels of pouring.

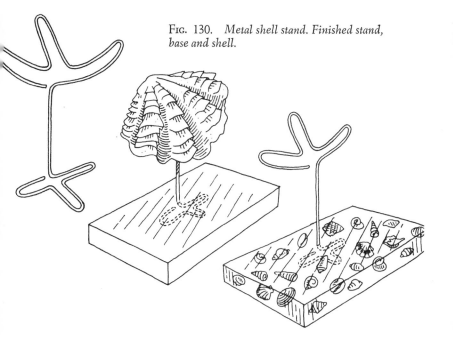

Fig. 130. *Metal shell stand. Finished stand,
base and shell.*

A SNAIL IN A SNAIL

A clear plastic snail is cast from a 4½-inch 3-D snail mold, and suspended in its middle is a brown-and-ivory-striped tree snail from the West Indies.

Tools and Materials

Measuring cup, disposable mixing cups, wooden coffee stirrers, eye-dropper, black felt-tipped marker, long pin, thread, wire or nail.

A 3-D snail mold 4½ inches high, a brown-and-ivory Tree Snail Shell (*Pleurodonte marginella*), liquid resin plus hardener. A sheet of mylar.

Steps

1. Make a cardboard box support for the mold. Also check the surface of your working table to be sure it is level. (See page 166.)

2. Mix enough clear resin for the first ¼-inch layer of pouring and to fill half the cavity in the shell.

3. When dry, add a ⅜-inch layer of clear plastic to the mold and fill the shell cavity.

4. The shell should center on the shell design of the snail, so keep adding ⅜-inch layers of resin until there is a sticky layer into which you can press one narrow edge of the shell. The spiral, brown-and-white design should face outward. You may have to hold the shell in position with a piece of string temporarily attached to the shell and to horizontal wire or nail at the top of the mold. (See "A Shimmering Pyramid," Step 4, page 182.)

5. When the resin is hard, pour in the next layer and let harden. Remove the string and continue pouring and hardening layers until you have filled the mold.

6. When the top is tacky and the mold still warm, remove the casting.

7. Rest the casting upright on its bottom area on a sheet of mylar and let harden overnight.

Variations

Resin can be tinted a light tan or yellow. Several small snail shells can be embedded at different levels.

FIG. 131.   A Tree Snail Shell from Puerto Rico.

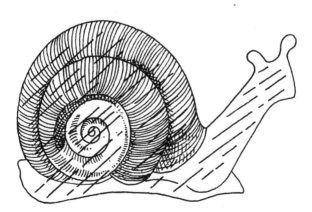

FIG. 132.   Snail molded from liquid resin.

AN ICY CHRISTMAS TREE

Fill an 8-inch, 3-D Christmas tree mold with clear casting resin to look like ice sculpture. Embed small, colorful shells near the points of the branches—black-and-white striped nerites, zebras, white wentletraps and a small Star Shell placed at the top.

Tools and Materials

Measuring cup, disposable mixing cups, wooden coffee stirrers, eye-dropper, black felt-tipped marker, long pin, a piece of thin stiff wire, a flashlight.

An 8-inch, 3-D Christmas tree mold. Tiny varieties of patterned shells such as Zebra Nerite (*Puperita pupa*), Spotted Nerite (*Neritina punctulata*), some of the Periwinkles (*Littorina*), Long-spined Star Shell (*Astraea phoebia*), Dove Shells (*Anachis*)—look through your collection and make your choice. Liquid resin plus hardener. A sheet of mylar.

Steps

1. Make the support for the mold. (See page 166.)
2. Spread out your shells, pick the ones you want to use and plan just where you will embed them, working out the pouring schedule of the resin and the placing of the shells.
3. Mix enough resin for the ¼-inch first layer and also to fill the cavities of the shells.
4. Follow your plan of ⅜-inch layers of resin, placement of shells, drying, then pouring again until the top opening is level. Use the fine wire to place the shells in position. A flashlight may come in handy as you will not be able to see through the opaque mold.
5. When the top is dry or slightly tacky and the mold still warm, peel off the flexible material. (See page 169.) Stick star shell on top.
6. Try not to handle the casting too much as you set it upright on a sheet of mylar to harden overnight.

Variation

Light green color can be added to the clear resin.

FIG. 133. *Black-and-white Nerite Shells.*

FIG. 134. *Finished casting of Christmas tree mold with shells showing through.*

CAPTURE A TIDE POOL

Cast a large pouring resin form, either in a round pie pan with slanting sides or a cake pan with straight sides. Embed all sorts of shells, seaweed, a starfish known as Sunflower Star (*Pycnopodia helianthoides*) and a bit of sand, then hang it all on the wall or place it on a low table where you can look down into the depths.

Tools and Materials

Measuring cup, disposable mixing cups, wooden coffee stirrers, eyedropper, black felt-tipped marker, long pin.

Metal mold, paste mold-release, liquid resin plus hardener, a sheet of mylar and all sorts of sea things as described in the first paragraph.

Steps

1. Make sure your working area is level. Rub mold-release on metal pie or cake pan.

2. Mix the amount of clear resin, or resin faintly tinged with blue or green, for the first ¼-inch layer. Also fill any Snail Shell cavities part way with the resin. Let everything harden. Finish filling shell cavities so that no air bubbles will escape into the casting.

3. Start building up the layers in the metal pan, adding part of your decorations to each ¼- to ⅜-inch layer, overlapping some materials but also leaving some areas clear to approximate water. Use the long pin to position the shells. Your design should not be overcrowded. All material should face downward as the "bottom" of the casting will become the top when it is turned out.

4. The whole plaque will be about 1 inch thick. The last smooth covering layer is ¼ inch thick.

5. Let harden until the surface is hard but the form still warm, then turn out on a sheet of mylar and let harden overnight.

6. If using as a wall plaque, attach one of the stick-on metal loops, or epoxy on a loop of heavy cord. Try to place the hanger behind a shell so as not to spoil the clear look of the casting.

BEACH COINAGE PENDANT

Try embedding a small Sand Dollar (*Mellita quinquiesperforata* or *Dendraster excentricus*) in a round mold to make a pendant.

Tools and Materials

Measuring cup, disposable mixing cups, wooden coffee stirrers, eye-dropper, black felt-tip marker and long pin.

A disk-shaped mold 2⅜ inches in diameter and 1⅛ inches deep. A sand dollar or Keyhole Urchin (one of the several kinds found on the beaches of both coasts). Liquid resin plus hardener. A sheet of mylar. You will also need a cord or chain and perhaps a ring catch and jump ring.

Steps

1. The disk should not be more than ⅝ inch deep, so mark the outside of the mold with a black felt-tipped pen.

2. Mix and pour in the first thin layer of resin, about ³⁄₁₆ inch.

3. When this layer is almost dry, add the sand dollar with its best side down and pour in the next layer of resin to just cover it. Pour very carefully over a mixing stick, allowing the material to flow under the sand dollar. Watch for bubbles and prick any that form. Cover the sand dollar and let the resin harden.

4. Add the final layer of resin which should be ³⁄₁₆ inch.

5. When the top layer is hard or just tacky, remove the casting from the mold and let it dry, tacky side up, on a sheet of mylar.

6. When thoroughly hard, make a hole at the top from front to back with a hot, thin nail. Run the cord through and tie a knot at the top of the disk. Add a catch at the ends of the cord, following directions given for "A Cord Full of Cowries" ("Variations," page 118).

CRYSTAL MADELEINES

Clear crystal forms baked in madeleine pans, with or without an embedded shell, will probably make Proust turn over in his grave, but they are fun and delightful as small, shell-shaped paperweights, mobile hangers or wind chimes.

Tools and Materials

Madeleine pans, clear baking crystals, aluminum foil, and small bright-colored Scallop Shells (*Pectens*).

Steps

1. Preheat oven to 375°.

2. Put the madeleine pan on a baking sheet. Half fill the bottoms of

199

the cavities with colorless baking crystals. Put a shell, face down, in the middle of each, then add crystals until each cavity is full.

3. Put the pan into the oven until the surface is smooth—approximately 30 minutes. Take out and let your castings cool in molds. The plastic will shrink away from the molds, and when they are cold you can turn the castings out onto a sheet of aluminum foil.

Variations

With a thin, hot nail make a hole at the top of each shell form, and use them as the components of a mobile, hanging them on nylon fishing line from wire crosspieces.

Place three or four forms, curved side down, in a straight line—tops to bottoms. Support each curve with a piece of Plasti-Tak to hold it steady. Stretch a length of nylon fishing line tautly over the tops and hold in place with epoxy cement. Make several of these lines to hang from a small embroidery hoop as a wind chime; the number of lines depends on the size of the hoop. Cover the hoop with nylon line looped over and over in a bottonhole loop.

Colored crystals can be used in place of clear crystals.

The shell-like forms can be added with epoxy cement as surface decorations to flat-cast resin tiles. Use as paperweights. They can also be used for decorating commercial plastic photo cubes.

FIG. 135. *Large Sunflower Starfish* (Pycnopodia helianthoides).

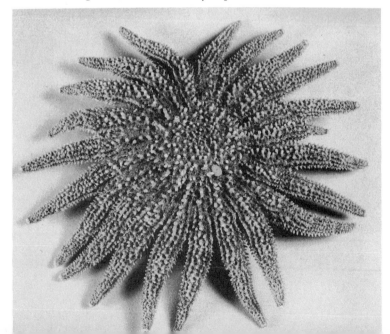

Fig. 136. *A sand dollar and keyhole urchin.*

Fig. 137. *Finished beach coinage pendant (page 198).*

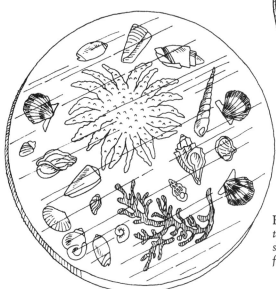

Fig. 138. *Large, round tide pool scene of shells, seaweed and sunflower star (page 198).*

Fig. 139.   *Madeleine pan being filled with clear baking crystals (page 199).*

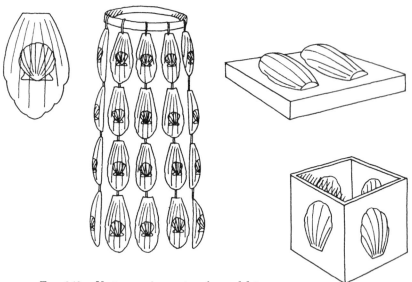

Fig. 140.   *Various projects using the madeleine pan molds: wind chime, box and tile (page 200).*

COQUINA DUCK PIN

This is a project that takes a bit of patience, but the result is fascinating. The small Coquina Shells (*Donax variabilis*), overlapping like feathers, are held in position by the baking crystals—the whole affair arranged in a small, duck-shaped cookie mold.

Tools and Materials

Clear baking crystals, Coquina Shells, a duck-shaped cookie cutter, aluminum foil, baking sheet, a pinback plus epoxy cement.

Steps

1. Put aluminum foil on baking sheet and place the cookie cutter on the foil.

2. Arrange the Coquina Shells inside the duck form with the convex curve against the foil. Overlap the shells slightly—the long edges should face toward the back of the duck (see Fig. 142).

3. Dribble clear baking crystals into the mold very carefully so as not to disturb the shells. Fill mold with a ¼-inch depth of crystals.

4. Put the baking sheet in the pre-heated 375° oven until the surface of the plastic is smooth and clear. Cool in the mold. Turn out on a sheet of aluminum foil.

5. Add a bar pinback to the clear plastic, using epoxy cement.

Caution: You may have to set the heat at 325° and bake the plastic a little longer, as the shells are unprotected and might be affected by the heat. You can also bake the material a shorter time until the surface is just bubbly. Then let cool and turn out of the mold.

Fig. 141. *Duck cookie cutter with and without baking crystals.*

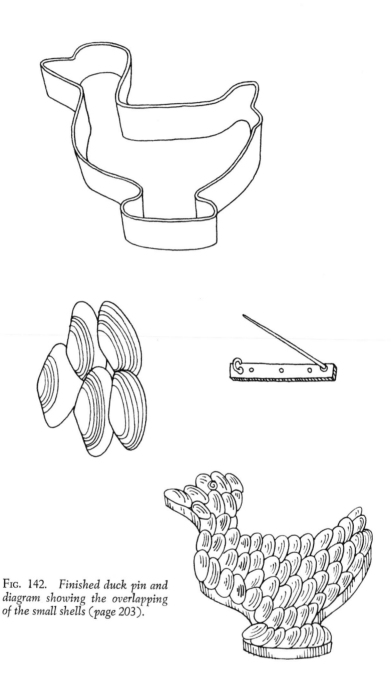

Fig. 142. *Finished duck pin and diagram showing the overlapping of the small shells (page 203).*

A TILED MIRROR FRAME

Try baking small, square or oblong plastic tiles with shells embedded to frame a small mirror. This makes a charming wall decoration.

Tools and Materials

Clear baking crystals, small square or oblong metal molds for tile shapes, aluminum foil, baking sheet, shells and a small, framed mirror.

Steps

1. Make sure the frame of the mirror is a smooth flat surface, and covered with flat white paint.

2. You will also have to plan the tile size as against the mirror frame size, or the frame size against the size of the metal forms you can find. Forms can also be made from several thicknesses of aluminum foil folded carefully to size and shape, and placed on a baking sheet. You can also make oblong shapes together with square ones (see Fig. 144).

3. Once these two variables have been adjusted, start collecting flat shells and planning your design. Shells need to be fairly thin as the thickness of baking crystal projects is about ¼ inch.

4. Fill forms with ⅛ inch of crystals, arrange shells, add the second ⅛-inch layer and place in the oven.

5. When top is shiny, remove and let cool, then turn out the tiles. If you have made aluminum foil forms, peel off the foil when the plastic is cool.

6. Working on a flat surface, apply epoxy cement to the frame and place tiles in position. Put weights, such as books, all around the frame on top of the tiles and let stay undisturbed for 24 hours.

Variations

Use light-colored crystals, choosing colors that match or contrast your room furnishings.

When filling the forms, add a darker color around the edges as a border. The colors will not mix into each other and you will have a frame around each tile.

Instead of shells use sea horses, starfish or seaweed.

Use as a picture frame around a single-shell block print on paper or cloth. (See Chapter 7.)

FIG. 143. *A lavender and rust Fan Shell* (Pecten ziczac).

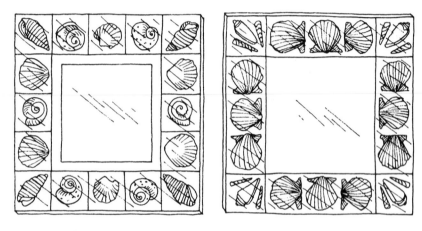

FIG. 144. *Several designs for the tiled-mirror frame* (*page 205*).

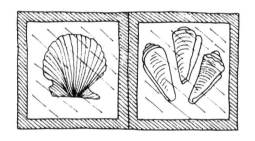

INTERCHANGEABLE FORMS

Now it's one thing, now it's another. Small shapes—rounds, squares, diamonds—some formed in pans or cookie molds, others in aluminum foil molds. These shapes become pendants, necklaces, key ring decorations, mobile components, wall hangings. Let your imagination go!

Tools and Materials

Clear or colored transparent baking crystals, plus assorted shells and molds, aluminum foil, baking sheet, chains, jewelry findings, cord, nylon fishing line and wire.

Steps

1. Clean shells, and dry well.
2. Embed a sliced Murex Shell section in a rectangle of light green or yellow, as a pendant. You can also add a row of black-and-white Zebra Shells (*Purperita pupa*) at the top and bottom of the rectangle.
3. Small squares and circles, each with a Jingle Shell (*Anomia simplex*) embedded, are pierced top and bottom with a thin, hot nail. Add jump rings that are linked to sections of fine chain. Alternate chain and plastic forms for a necklace or a belt.
4. Stick small and large forms, with shells embedded in the plastic or placed on top, on heavy cord alternating with shells to make a wall hanging strung on a bamboo pole.
5. Use embedded forms for key ring decorations.
6. Forms are linked together with jump rings to create bracelets fastened with jump catches.
7. Solidly fill a round form with Screw Shells (*Terebra*) with their points facing inward and almost touching. Use as a center pendant for a necklace.

Fig. 145.   *Jingle Shells* (Anomia simplex).

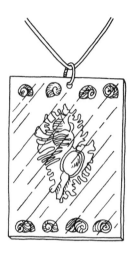

Fig. 146.   *Several designs of jewelry made with shells and baking crystals* (page 207).

6

Making Cast Shell Forms
from Molds

MAKING MOLDS is an ideal way to develop designs if one has only a few shells, as they can be used and re-used in a number of different projects. Any number of castings can be made from an individual mold and the finished product can be made of clay, plastic or plaster of Paris.

What starts out as a simple tile design to hang on the wall can be multiplied to border a mirror. By casting four decorative tiles plus one plain one, you can make an open box for a plant holder or a container for nuts or candy—and by adding a sixth tile the whole thing becomes a covered box.

Some designs have real shells incorporated on the surface of the casting, others will be decorated with a raised-shell casting or a sunken shell—intaglio—design or a combination of both, giving a negative and positive approach.

You can add color to the casting material or add color on the surface, or just use the color of the casting material—the stark white of plaster of Paris, the warm earth browns of clay, or the clear transparency of plastic.

TOOLS

Tools are extremely simple, consisting of household or kitchen tools such as: *large spoons* and *teaspoons;* a long, narrow *spatula;* a glass or

209

aluminum *measuring cup;* wooden *coffee stirrers* or *tongue depressors.*
Metal or plastic containers which can be *coffee tins* or *plastic freezer*
containers for mixing plaster of Paris. *Wood file* and *paint brush.*

MATERIALS

Shells of various sizes and types. Wooden, cardboard or plastic *boxes*
of the necessary sizes to hold the molding material. Strips of 1½- to 2-
inch-wide *wooden lath* of various lengths to make frames to hold molding material. Mold materials, which are *sand, plaster of Paris* and *liquid-
rubber mold compound.* Also *clay* and *plasticene,* which are used as mold
caulking and forming materials. *Sandpaper* for cleaning any rough edges
of the casting. *Shellac* and *alcohol* for sealing plaster of Paris molds.
Mold soap, mold-release paste and *petroleum jelly* to facilitate the removal of casting from the mold.

MAKING A SAND MOLD

First, decide what size the finished casting will be, then find a cardboard, wooden or plastic box of the right size. It should be deep enough
so that the shell to be cast does not come too close to the bottom when
pushed into the sand, which would allow the liquid plaster of Paris to
break through the bottom of the mold. Allow ½ to ¾ inch between the
top of the sand and the top of the box. This will be the depth of the
finished tile.

Before filling the box with sand, decide on your design—which shells
you will use and how they will be placed. Make a drawing to size on a
sheet of paper.

Now make the mold. You can use any sand, fine or coarse—beach
sand, builder's sand or sand bought at a pet shop. Moisten the sand

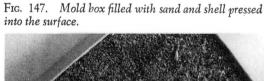

Fig. 147. *Mold box filled with sand and shell pressed
into the surface.*

thoroughly; it should be damp all through, and firm enough to pack into the box. If it is too wet it will soak the sides of the box; if too dry the sand will not hold a clean impression of the molded material. Press down evenly and level the top surface, using your hand, a spatula, a length of lath or a wooden ruler.

The next step is to press your shells into the sand, following the design you have worked out on the same-size sheet of paper. Push the objects into the sand cleanly and firmly so that the outlines will be sharp and clear. Lift each one out, trying not to disturb the walls of the mold. If, for instance, you are making an impression of a Cockle Shell, you may want to stick a looped piece of tape onto the convex side to act as a handle in pulling out the shell. You are now ready to add the casting material.

MAKING THE CASTING

To mix the plaster of Paris for a casting, you will have to judge roughly how much water and plaster you will need. There are formulas but if you are making an irregular casting all simple arithmetic falls apart. Here it is anyway: two cups of water plus 1½ cups of plaster of Paris will fill a volume of approximately 35 cubic inches. (This amount is achieved by multiplying length x height x width. But if you mix too little plaster of Paris you can always mix more and add to the casting. If you mix too much, just throw it away—it's that simple. No matter what amount you are mixing, follow the same proportions of water and plaster.

So, onward. Measure and pour the water into a mixing bowl, plastic container or metal coffee can. If the plaster is sort of lumpy, sift it over the surface of the water. Let stand for a moment, then mix carefully, using your hands and squeezing out any lumps. Do not lift hands up and down, but move them very gently through the liquid so that air bubbles

Fig. 148. *Mold box and sand showing impression of the shell.*

will not be introduced into the mixture. When well mixed and the consistency of cream, rinse off your hands in rapidly flowing water so as to carry the plaster through the sink trap. Some craftspeople keep a bucket of water handy for rinsing off hands and tools, letting it stand so that any plaster sinks to the bottom. The water is poured off and the residue thrown away in the trash.

Now, using a teaspoon, *dribble, do not pour,* the plaster mixture into the hollows in the sand mold, being careful not to disturb the walls of the shell impressions. As the hollows are filled, work outward over the flat surface, slowly adding plaster. If you pour the plaster you will just create deep "pour holes" in the sand, spoiling the design. After everything is well covered, you can slowly pour the rest of the plaster into the mold in one corner, until the mold is full.

Let the plaster set undisturbed for about 30 minutes to 1 hour. It will be cold to the touch, then warm, then cold again. Place the mold on a tray or a table covered with clean newspaper. Peel off one side of the cardboard box. Then peel off the rest of the cardboard. The sand will leak out of the sides and bottom as you work. (The sand can be re-used to make other molds.) Lift out the mold and turn it over, letting it dry upright for another hour with the sand still clinging to the plaster.

When the mold is completely dry, brush the sand away with a soft brush. You will find that some of the sand will be embedded in your casting, giving the surface the sandy look of a "sand casting."

If you are on a beach, you can make your casting right there by forming a mold within an area braced by four thin sticks of wood or lath. Do this casting on a sunny day and you will find that the plaster will dry rapidly. When the casting has hardened, take the wood away carefully, scoop up the design and turn over and let dry thoroughly, then brush off the excess sand.

MAKING A RUBBER MOLD

An easy-to-make rubber mold has one of the advantages of sand casting: you can choose a shell that has *undercutting*—that is, a part that cuts back under the top surface. A rubber mold can be eased off the original object, pulled up and out from the undercut parts of the shell. In addition, every finely modeled or complicated surface can be reproduced perfectly, and a number of materials can be used for the final casting: plaster of Paris, a cold liquid metal sold as liquid solder, and liquid casting resin. The third great advantage is that the mold is re-usable.

Cover the object to be cast with Vaseline, green soap, or Pliatex separator, but be sure to use *only* the protective coating recommended by the manufacturer of the liquid rubber product. Use a soft brush which can get into cracks and around points. Be sure that the covering is a *thin skin* over the shell so that the details are not lost.

There are a number of liquid rubber materials sold in art and craft stores, including Pliatex and Rubamold, two products that I have used; it is best to follow the manufacturer's directions for applying and drying their material. Some products are immediately useable, such as the two mentioned, others come in two components to be mixed together. One procedure, though, is used for all: the material is applied in thin successive layers—from 6 to 16 or more—depending on the object to be covered and the weight of the final casting material. Allow each layer to dry before applying the next one. In the case of rounded snail-type shells you will not be casting the whole shell, but only half or three-quarters of it to be used as a flat-bottomed decorative object. In all cases the mold should be a minimum of ¼ inch thick.

Since the mold will be following the curved area of a shell, the last layer or two should be a little thicker than the first ones so that the curve is smooth and any protrusions on the shell are then leveled in this thickened surface. This will aid in supporting the weight of the casting material and form a more solid base.

Once the last coat of rubber material has been applied, let dry for one to three days. Before removing the shell, hollow out a section of styrofoam to act as a support for the mold and to assure a level surface for pouring. Once this is done, ease the mold off the shell. Coat mold with whatever material the manufacturer recommends before pouring in the casting material. Now pour in the casting material, let harden and peel off the mold. Re-use mold as often as you need it.

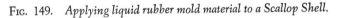

FIG. 149. *Applying liquid rubber mold material to a Scallop Shell.*

MAKING A PLASTER OF PARIS MOLD

In contrast to a sand mold, a plaster of Paris mold is a permanent one from which you can make many castings. It is ideal for making tiles of either plaster of Paris, clay or liquid casting resin. The tiles can be used separately or formed into boxes or open containers.

Positive Mold for Tiles

First, decide on the tile shape, size and thickness—a minimum of ½ inch. The pattern slab is then formed of wet clay from which you will make the plaster of Paris mold. (See the directions further on in this chapter for handling clay.) Press wet shells into the rolled clay to make the design (see "Making a Sand Mold" in this chapter). But be absolutely sure that there are no undercuttings in the impressions as this will mean that you will not be able to pull the mold away from casting—they will be locked together. With sand you just brushed the mold away; plaster of Paris is a solid, hard material.

In this plaster of Paris *positive mold,* the shell design in the mold will be raised so that your final casting will have an intaglio design—one that is sunk into the surface area. The advantage of this method is that only one or two shells are needed to make a design; they are repeatedly pressed into the moist pattern slab over which the plaster of Paris mold is cast. (See Fig. 150.)

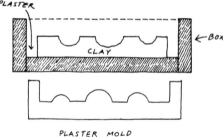

Fig. 150.   *Positive plaster of Paris mold cast over an imprinted clay tile.*

Negative or Intaglio Mold for Tiles

Here are three ways of making a *negative or intaglio* plaster of Paris mold in which the shell design is hollowed out of the plaster mold, so that when the final clay or liquid casting resin is put into the mold, the final casting will be in *relief*—that is, the shell design stands out from the background in convex form.

First, pour a ¾- to 1-inch layer of plaster of Paris into a wooden, cardboard or plastic box and let it almost harden. Thinly cover the surface of the shells with Vaseline or some other petroleum jelly and place them, convex side down, on the top surface of the almost hardened plaster of Paris. The shells should be arranged in the final design. Spoon plaster around the shells and up to their top edges if they are bivalves, halfway up if they are of the snail type, being careful that there is no undercutting on the shells and that you will be able to lift them out easily from the hardened plaster, which will shrink away a bit from the shell surfaces as it dries. Try also to choose shells of the same depth. If not, plan on two pourings—the deeper shells first placed in position, a thin layer of plaster added, hardened, then the shallower shells added, and so filling the mold to the proper level for all the shells. (See Fig. 151a.)

When the plaster is stiff, remove from the mold box and let dry until hard. Remove the shell models as well.

This type of mold is ideal for making rolled clay flat tiles or box covers, or long tiles to be wrapped around cans or bottles to form cylindrical vases.

The second method is used to make a mold for casting clear pouring resin or plaster of Paris. Here you will have to add a 1-inch "shoulder" to your mold all around the edges to contain the liquid resin. (See Fig. 151b.) Plan your shell design so that it is contained within an area which allows for a 1-inch margin all around the edges. Make the mold as above and when the plaster is almost hard, place a cardboard hollow-box shape like a fence on top of the mold at the 1-inch margin line. Add a thin roll of clay or plasticene on the inside base of the cardboard fence to keep the plaster from running into the design already hardened. Fill the outside margin with the plaster to a ¾-inch depth and let harden thoroughly. Remove the inner cardboard and protective roll of clay or plasticene, then remove the whole mold from the master mold box.

The third method of negative- or intaglio-mold making involves placing a ¾-inch-thick slab of moist, rolled clay in the bottom of the mold box, allowing for a 1-inch margin between the tile and the sides of the mold box. (See Fig. 151c.) Place the Vaseline-covered clam-type or *Pecten* Shells in position on the clay, *convex sides up,* pressing them slightly into the clay to hold them in position. Pour the liquid plaster around the shells, covering them to a depth of ¾ to 1 inch. Let the plaster harden. Turn out the mold, strip off the clay and remove all the shells, letting the mold stand until hard and dry. This third method can be used for casting resin.

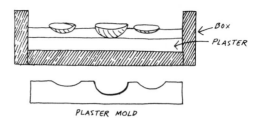

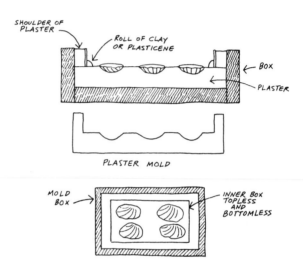

FIG. 151a.   Plaster of Paris negative mold—method 1.

FIG. 151b.   Plaster of Paris negative mold—method 2.

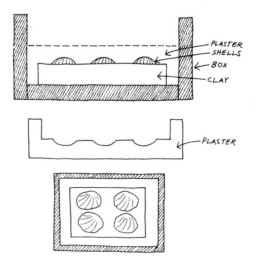

FIG. 151c.   Plaster of Paris negative mold—method 3.

If you cannot find a box of the right size for either a positive or negative mold, then place the moist clay pattern slab on a baking sheet or large plastic tray (see Fig. 152). Form the four sides around the slab with strips of wood lath held in position (*on the outside only*) with coils of clay or plasticene, so that the liquid plaster will not flow out from under the side walls of the mold.

Mix plaster according to directions at the beginning of this chapter and pour into the mold. You do not have to be careful in pouring as the damp clay slab is solid. But pour gently along a piece of lath or wooden stirrer so as to prevent bubbles in the mold material. Let harden. The mold will shrink slightly away from the boards. Remove caulking and boards, turn mold upright and remove clay. Let everything dry well. After the mold is thoroughly dry, wash it out under running water to remove bits of clay which might still be sticking to the plaster. Again let dry. Then remove any rough edges with sandpaper.

All of these plaster of Paris molds are ideal for tile designs cast in clay, liquid casting resin or plaster of Paris. You can also make molds of single shells to be cast as just individual models for various projects.

If any of the molds are to be used for casting plaster of Paris or liquid casting resin, waterproof with several thin coats of shellac thinned with alcohol in the proportion of one-half shellac and one-half alcohol. Let dry between coats and sandpaper to a smooth surface. Mold should not be waterproofed if it is to be used for a clay casting.

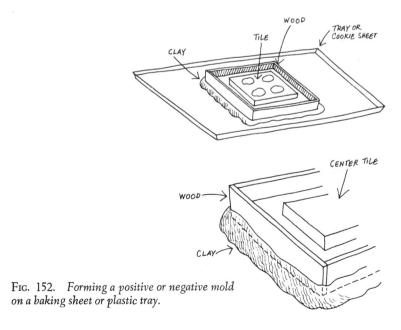

Fig. 152. *Forming a positive or negative mold on a baking sheet or plastic tray.*

MAKING THE CASTING IN A PLASTER MOLD

Plaster of Paris

Mix the plaster according to directions at the beginning of this chapter. Coat the inside of the mold with mold soap which can be bought in any ceramic supply shop. Pour in the plaster very carefully so as not to create any bubbles. Tap the outside of the mold sharply to bring bubbles to the surface and prick them with a needle. Let liquid harden, ½ to 1 hour, and turn out the casting to dry on a flat surface, right side up. Repeat process for as many tiles as you need.

Liquid Casting Resin

For a liquid casting resin tile, you will use the mold that has been waterproofed. Rub the surface with mold-release paste. Mix the resin according to the manufacturer's directions, being very careful to avoid stirring air into the mixture. Pour slowly into the mold over the flat side of a wide spatula to minimize the forming of bubbles. Fill the mold only part way as the resin builds up heat in drying, and too deep a layer could impede the hardening of the material. Layers of ½ to ⅜ inch are best. If your mold is very deep, you will be pouring several layers. See the beginning of Chapter 5 for detailed descriptions of mixing and pouring clear liquid casting resin.

WORKING WITH CLAY

Tools

Rolling pin and *board, pointed, small paring knife, baking sheet, oven thermometer, wire modeling tools, brushes,* two *15-inch strips of wooden lath, small sponge, wire, small plastic containers, metal measuring spoons, small glass jars, wooden stirrers* and *large mixing spoons.*

Materials

There are two types of *clay*. The regular "classic" type is fired (baked) in a high temperature kiln, cooled, glazed, and fired again at the same high heat to melt and harden the surface covering. The other is a more modern kind which can be baked in the kitchen oven at 250°. The glaze finish is air-dried. As this type of glazed clay is not waterproof, you will have to paint the inside of a container with a *clear, waterproof resin* if any material is to be put inside it. But if you are a beginner, I would advise this second type of clay as it will achieve the results you want very quickly with the minimum of supplies and expense. *Della Robbia Miracle Clay* is a lovely soft brown color and the glazes are both *opaque* and *transparent*. *Ceraclay* is a gray clay, smoother in texture and the glazes are also opaque and transparent.

Directions

Remove enough clay from the container to fill the tile form and knead it on a smooth, waterproof surface until all bubbles are out of the clay. Bubbles will cause your piece to explode during baking. Press the clay into the *untreated* mold, smoothing off the top. When the clay has shrunk away from the sides, turn out the casting. You can make one or two more tiles before having to let the mold dry out—it is the absorption of water by the porous plaster which dries out the clay.

Let tiles dry for several days until hard, then bake for ½ to ¾ hour, but follow the manufacturer's directions for the length of baking time.

If you are putting several tiles together to form a container, they should be joined when the clay is almost hard—that is, hard enough so that the clay tile can be handled without bending, but not dry-hard. Scratch the areas to be joined with the point of a knife, and add a thickish slurry made with clay and water (called slip) over the scratched surface. Put the pieces together and brace them until dry. You may also want to smooth in a thin, thin coil of clay along the inside seams. Make a flat, plain tile for the bottom by rolling out the clay with a rolling pin on a plastic-covered surface, then cutting it to size with a pointed knife.

After the clay has been baked, mix the glaze according to the manufacturer's directions and apply it. I have found that more satisfactory results are achieved by air-drying than by baking the glaze in the oven. The air-drying will take several days, depending on the weather.

SUGGESTIONS FOR WORKING WITH CLAY

Clay is an essential part of the mold-making of tiles, but it is also a material used for bowls, boxes and vases which are decorated with cast shells and impressed shell designs. Here are simple guides for working with clay as a basic material in the projects which are detailed later on in this chapter.

1. When making unmolded slabs and tiles, roll out the clay on a plastic-covered surface, placing a strip of ½-inch lath on each side as tracks for the rolling pin. This will automatically give you an even depth for the slab of clay. With a pin prick out any air bubbles or blisters that form on the surface.

2. Clay slabs can be wrapped around a bottle or jar to form a cylinder, with a circle of clay as a base. Slabs are draped over the bottom of a bowl and pressed closely, then dried until stiff enough to remove without damaging.

3. Separate clay forms are attached to each other with slip, which is a thick, creamy liquid made from clay and water mixed together. This acts like glue. Clay pieces to be attached to each other must be of the same moistness and should not be too dry, but they should be stiff enough to hold their shape and not collapse when handled.

4. The potter's term "leather hard" describes clay that is well along to being dry enough for trimming, carving, and smoothing with a wet sponge.

5. All clay must be absolutely dry before it is baked. This means several days of just sitting in a room; the length of time depends on the atmosphere.

6. When baking, clay should be put into a kitchen oven at 150° with the door left wide open for 30 minutes so that all moisture will leave the "pot." Then increase heat to 250° for 30 to 45 minutes, leaving the door open only about 2 inches.

7. If any moisture has been left in the pot, or if there are any bubbles in the dried clay, your piece will shatter or crack as the steam or air expands and attempts to escape through the hardened surface.

8. After baking, cool the piece slowly by opening the door of the oven and letting the pot remain in the cooling oven.

9. Glazes are then applied and allowed to air dry. Sometimes this can take a week if the weather is humid, but in a heated room in the winter this time is shortened.

Other techniques and suggestions will be contained in individual projects as special approaches are needed. Clay is easy to work with, but it cannot be forced. In bending the material, one works carefully, allowing it to adjust to a new shape. If it cracks, put water into the crack and press and smooth it together. When a project has to be left partially completed, cover with a plastic bag to keep the clay moist until you can work on it again. If, while you are working, the clay tends to dry out, moisten the surface with a damp sponge, but never let it get too wet and muddy or it will collapse.

Several of the projects in this chapter are clay-molded ones, and each is a basic description of one design. But shapes, sizes and objects can be changed and interchanged as you develop many other ways to use clay, shells and molds for new and unusual decorations.

A PLASTER SCALLOP PAPERWEIGHT

This is the simplest of all sand castings and should be tried first, as the scallop is a simple impression with bold outlines.

Tools and Materials

Spatula or a length of lath or ruler, spoon, measuring cup, plastic bowl or container. Wooden, plastic or cardboard mold box.

Sand, plaster of Paris, plus a large Coquille St. Jacques Scallop (*Pecten*) baking shell.

Fɪɢ. 153.   *White Coquille St. Jacques Scallop Shell.*

Steps

1. In choosing the box for the casting, allow 1½ inches all around the shell which is 5 inches wide and 4½ inches long, so you will want a box 8 x 7½ inches. The sand will be 3½ to 4 inches deep, and the area between the top of the sand and the top of the box will be ¾ inch, which is the depth of the finished scallop tile.

2. Fill the box with damp sand.

3. Mix plaster of Paris.

4. Press shell into the center of the sand, convex side down, then remove without disturbing the impression.

5. Carefully dribble the plaster into the shell area, and gradually fill the mold up to the top of the box, or ¾ inch deep.

6. Let dry for an hour. If the box is a paper one, tear away the sides and carefully remove the casting. Turn it right side up and let it dry thoroughly, then brush off the excess sand with a soft brush.

Fig. 154.
Sandcasting of a plaster Scallop paperweight.

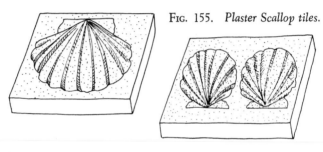

Fig. 155.   *Plaster Scallop tiles.*

Variations

You can also make a casting of the shell only, by filling the shell mold with plaster but not continuing over the flat surface of the sand.

Make several sandcastings of Scallop Shells, using one or two shells to make square- and oblong-tile wall decorations. By also using a larger casting box you can make a number of impressions and pourings of single shells at one time.

Try a Scotch bonnet or other shells on top of a tile.

If you are going to hang the tile on the wall, press a metal hanger into the almost-hard plaster of Paris.

A REAL SCALLOP PLAQUE

Try a combination of small, snow-white scallops held in a sandy background for a contrasting wall plaque.

Tools and Materials

Spatula or a length of lath or ruler, spoon, measuring cup, plastic bowl or container. Wooden, plastic or cardboard mold box.

Sand, plaster of Paris, plus two large Coquille St. Jacques Scallop (*Pecten*) baking shells.

Steps

1. Pack a 5 x 7½-inch box with sand to the depth of 2½ inches, making sure there is space at the top for a ¾-inch-deep tile base for the two shells.

2. Mix the plaster of Paris.

3. Press the two shells into the sand, curved side down, the hinge areas touching each other in the center of the rectangle. The edges of the shells should be just above the edge of the flat area of sand, so that the plaster will flow under a bit to hold the shells in place.

4. Fill the hollows of each shell with the plaster. Still pouring into the shell hollows, let the plaster flow over the flat area until it reaches a depth of ¾ inch.

5. Let the casting dry for about an hour. If the box is a paper one, tear away the sides and carefully remove the casting. Turn it right side up and let it dry thoroughly, then brush off the excess sand with a soft brush. The white shells will contrast with the sandy background as some sand will be embedded in the plaster.

6. If you are planning to use this design as a wall plaque, press a picture hanger into the tile surface when the plaster is thick but not completely hard. You can also use a soft-drink-can tab, slipping the tab part under the surface of the almost-hard plaster, leaving the circle exposed for hanging.

Fig. 156. *White Pacific Ocean Scallop Shells.*

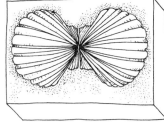

Fig. 157. *Shells embedded in plaster of Paris sandcasting.*

A MONSTER STARFISH

As a first project for a rubber mold, try a Bahamian Starfish, 6½ inches across and 1½ inches thick in the center. This makes a lovely paperweight or decoration. It is all spiny and webbed and sandy-colored, a magnificent creature to cast in plaster of Paris or casting resin.

Tools and Materials

Spoons, soft brush, wooden stirrers, mixing bowl or can, and a measuring cup. Rubber mold material, plaster of Paris, mold box, starfish, styrofoam.

Steps

1. Make the rubber mold. Since you will be casting with plaster of Paris which is heavy, try to make a fairly thick wall of rubber over the starfish, rounding out the top surfaces of the arms.

2. When the rubber has hardened well, and before removing the starfish, turn the whole thing over and trace the outline on a thick piece of styrofoam. Dig out the styrofoam to form a support for the mold. Remove the starfish and settle the rubber mold into the styrofoam. You can also sink the mold into a box of sand as a support, but be very careful that the sand does not get into the mold.

3. Mix, and pour the plaster of Paris into the mold. When hard, remove the mold by stretching it a little to release the casting.

4. Let the casting dry overnight.

Variations

Add dry poster color to the plaster before pouring so that the starfish will have a natural color, or make it an unreal wild color.

Try pouring liquid casting resin into the mold for a clear or colorful starfish paperweight. You can also embed a small starfish in the center of the casting.

Make a casting of a large sea urchin—spines removed—bringing the mold just beyond the beginning of the bottom curve so that it will be easy to remove it.

FIG. 158. *A monster starfish from Grand Bahama Island.*

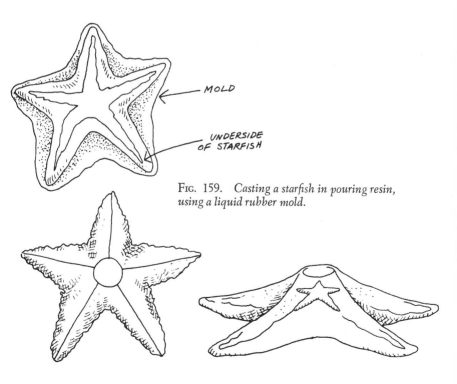

MOLD

UNDERSIDE
OF STARFISH

FIG. 159. *Casting a starfish in pouring resin,
using a liquid rubber mold.*

AN ALL-SORTS TILE

This is a piled-up design of several forms and sizes of shells, but all of them simple shapes—scallops, cockles and clam types. The center is the highest, blending out to shallow edges. Plan on an oblong design, 4 x 7 inches or more. Use as a table decoration, a paperweight or a wall plaque.

Tools and Materials

Spatula, or a length of lath or ruler, spoon, measuring cup, plastic bowl or container. Wooden, plastic or cardboard mold box.

Sand, plaster of Paris, and shells of your choice—see suggestions in the first paragraph.

Steps

1. Fill the mold box with dampened sand and press down well, smoothing off the top and allowing ¾ inch between the top of the sand and the box edge as the thickness of the tile. Make sure your working surface is level, so that the tile will be the same depth all around.

2. Mix plaster of Paris.

3. Starting in the center of the sand, scoop out the top surface into a shallow, curved depression. Press the center shell very deep, then press the other shells into the sand around the first one, pulling them out, brushing off any sand and then re-using them as models. In this way you can make a whole pattern with only four or five shells of different sizes and types.

4. When your design is complete, dribble in the plaster of Paris, being careful not to spoil the walls of the design. Fill the area right up to the top of the box. Add hanger pressed into plaster if this is to be a wall plaque.

5. Let harden for an hour. Remove box by tearing it away, lift out mold by the outside edges and turn it over so the right side is up. Let dry for several hours without touching the surface. When thoroughly dry, brush off the excess sand.

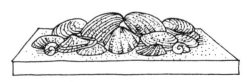

Fig. 160.   *Cockle Shells* (Trachycardium).

Fig. 161.   *Cockle Shells form the major part of this sand-molded plaster of Paris design.*

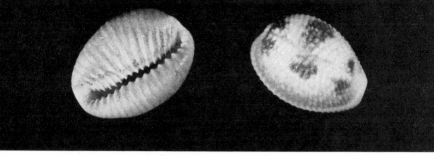

Fig. 162. *Coffee Bean Trivia* (Trivia pediculus).

ROLLED CLAY CYLINDER VASE

Make a tall, narrow cylinder of clay decorated with cast shells to hold sea grasses or other dried materials.

Tools and Materials

For the plaster of Paris mold you will need a spoon, measuring cup, and a plastic mixing bowl or container. Mold box of cardboard, wood or plastic.

Materials needed are: plaster of Paris, two types of shells—a moderate-size Little Yellow Cowrie (*Cypraea spurca*) or Coffee Bean (*Trivia pediculus*) and a Scallop Shell (*Pecten*)—several of each, depending on your design.

For the clay cylinder, gather together a rolling pin, small sponge, two pieces of wood lath ½ inch thick and 15 inches long, a pointed paring knife, small plastic container for mixing slip, and a baking sheet. Oven-baking clay, a wine or soda bottle with straight sides, a plastic cleaner's bag and air-dried glazes. And reread pages 219 and 220.

Steps

1. The general process involves making a flat plaster of Paris mold with an intaglio shell design into which clay will be rolled, and when partially dry, formed around a bottle to shape the cylinder.

2. First, wrap a sheet of paper around the bottle and cut away the excess at the joining edge, allowing for ½-inch extra on each end. This will be your pattern for the size of the negative plaster of Paris mold. Now make your mold. (See page 214.)

3. Roll clay into the mold with a rolling pin. It should be ½ inch thick above the mold surface. Trim edges even with sides of mold.

4. Let clay dry until it starts to shrink a bit, then turn out on a sheet of plastic with the design side facing up. This surface will have a raised

design of shells. Once the clay is stiff enough to handle, *but not too stiff to bend,* wrap it around the bottle, design side out, forming a cylinder. Fasten the edges together with slip.

5. Cut a circle of clay for the bottom of the cylinder.

6. Take the cylinder off the bottle before it is too hard, since in shrinking as it dries it will cling too tightly to the bottle and removal will be difficult.

7. Add the cylinder to the bottom circle with slip. Trim the top edge of the cylinder.

8. Finally, dry, bake and glaze the cylinder.

Variation

If you plan to make only one cylinder and have only one or two shells, you can press the shells into the rolled clay cylinder to make an intaglio design directly in the clay.

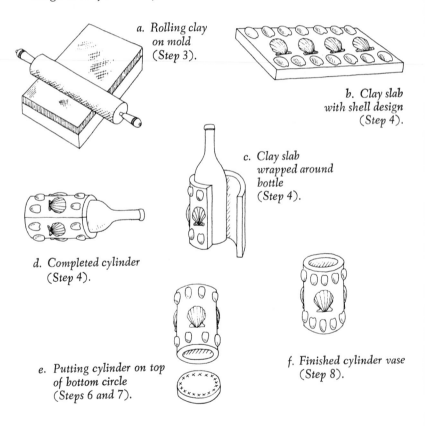

a. Rolling clay on mold (Step 3).

b. Clay slab with shell design (Step 4).

c. Clay slab wrapped around bottle (Step 4).

d. Completed cylinder (Step 4).

e. Putting cylinder on top of bottom circle (Steps 6 and 7).

f. Finished cylinder vase (Step 8).

Fig. 163. *Finished clay cylinder.*

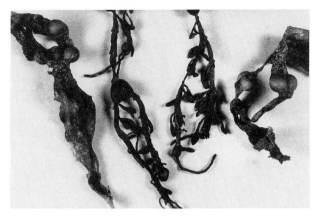

Fig. 164. *Dried seaweed.*

SLAB BOX OR CONTAINER

This is an oblong clay container or box with an intaglio seaweed or shell design—or a combination of both—imprinted on the surface. The glaze is the color or colors of your choice; it can be as subtle or as bright as you wish.

Tools and Materials

To work the clay you'll need a rolling pin, and two pieces of lath ½ inch thick and 15 inches long, a pointed paring knife, small sponge, a small plastic container for mixing and holding slip, a ruler, assorted brushes, stirrers, small containers for glazes and a baking sheet.

As materials you'll need oven-baking clay and air-dried glazes, as well as shells and seaweed chosen for their sharp imprints and recognizable forms. You'll need only one or two of each as you can repeat the models, the design being an intaglio one. Reread pages 219 and 220.

Steps

1. Plan the length, width and height of your container, and make a paper pattern for width and length pieces, as well as for the bottom. If you are planning on a cover, it will be the same size as the bottom.

2. For starters, let's plan on a container that is 3½ inches high, 4 inches wide and 6 inches long. This will mean that your side pattern will be 3 inches square, the front and back 3 inches high and 6 inches long, the bottom is 4 x 6 inches. The seeming discrepancy in height measurement is accounted for by the thickness of the clay bottom—½ inch. The overlapping front and back slabs account for ½ inch on each side, equaling 1 inch.

3. Roll out the clay, put patterns on top, and cut with a wet, sharp-

pointed knife: two short sides, two long pieces for sides, and one bottom plus one top if you are planning on a cover. Move each piece apart on the plastic surface.

4. After cutting, press the pattern of shells or seaweed into the clay. First, make a trial design on a piece of rolled scrap clay to see how hard and deep to press, and if the clay is the right consistency. If the clay is too soft, wait 10 or 15 minutes or more and try again. Wash shells off between pressings, and be sure that they are wet when you make an impression. Let sections dry until stiff enough to pick up without bending, but not too hard to put together.

5. Make a small container of slip and put the five sections together, first scratching the joints with the point of a sharp knife, adding slip and pressing together. Also, add a thin roll of clay along the inside joint, smoothing it into the rest of the clay. Smooth the outside of the joint so that it cannot be seen. Follow the diagram in Fig. 165 which shows how the sides and bottom are put together.

6. Cut the top edge at a 45° slant from outside to inside for a container project. Leave top edge flat if you are adding a cover.

7. When hard and dry, sandpaper away any bumps or rough areas, or go over the surface with a damp sponge.

8. Bake the clay.

9. Glaze the clay in the color of your choice. For this container, my choice is a transparent glaze with some green added so that the brown clay shows through and the green appears in the hollows and lightly on the flat surfaces—an almost no-color effect. Let dry until hard.

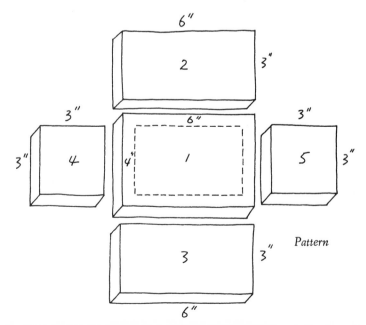

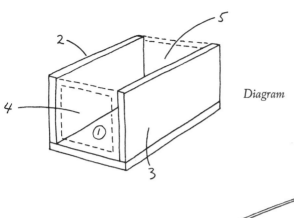

Diagram

Fig. 165. *Pattern and diagram for the slab box and drawings of the finished box.*

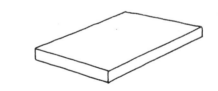

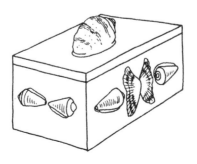

Fig. 166. *A white Scallop Shell from the Pacific Ocean.*
(*See also Fig. 139 for a madeleine mold.*)

MOLDED TILE TABLE TOP

Flat clay tiles for a table top are decorated along their outside edges with molded shells cast in a madeleine pan or Scallop-Shell mold.

Tools and Materials

Gather together a rolling pin, small sponge, two pieces of wood lath ½ inch thick and 15 inches long, a pointed paring knife, small plastic container for mixing and holding slip, assorted brushes, stirrers and mixing containers for the glazes, a madeleine pan and a baking sheet.

The materials include oven-baking clay and air-dried glazes, as well as tile adhesive and grout. Reread pages 219 and 220.

Steps

1. Decide on the number of tiles you will need to cover the top of a small table. Remember that the clay will shrink in drying, so allow for this. You might cut one tile to a measurement and let it dry, then bake it so that you will know the exact shrinkage. Do not make the tiles too large as your shell design will be lost. The center tiles will be plain, only the edging tiles have a design.

2. Roll out the clay ½ inch thick and cut out the tiles with a sharp, wet knife.

3. Fill the molds in a madeleine pan with clay, making one mold per tile and two for each corner tile. When they begin to shrink away from the sides, unmold. Or make a plaster Scallop Shell mold. (See page 221.)

4. Attach the molded shells to the tiles with slip and let tiles dry. When almost hard, smooth any rough spots with a damp sponge. Then dry until completely hard.

5. Bake the tiles, let cool and glaze in the color or colors of your choice.

6. Spread layer of tile adhesive on the table top and put tiles in position with a narrow space between each tile. Fill these spaces with grout from a tube. Let dry and your table is ready to use. An edging of wood, the depth of the tiles, placed around the outside of the table top is advisable, as this will protect the tiles from damage and give a finer finish to the edge.

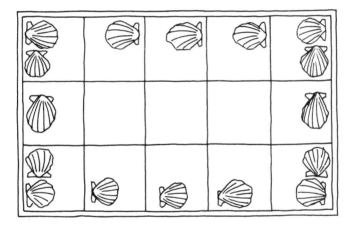

FIG. 167. *Drawing of tile-top table with tiles in place.*

Fig. 168. *A small starfish.*

A STARFISH DISH

Using the ancient Chinese technique of stencil and slip, a starfish design is raised up in the center of a shallow clay dish.

Tools and Materials

A rolling pin, small sponge, two pieces of wood lath ½ inch thick and 15 inches long, a pointed paring knife, small plastic container for mixing and holding slip, a shallow dish or saucer, jar, scissors, assorted brushes, stirrers and small containers for the glazes and a baking sheet.

Materials are oven-baking clay, air-dried glazes, a small starfish, stencil paper and a plastic cleaner's bag. Reread pages 219 and 220.

Steps

1. Roll out the clay in a ½-inch-thick slab.
2. Drape the clay over the outside of the saucer or shallow dish. Trim off the edges so they are even and let the clay dry. Support the dish on a jar so it is above your working surface.
3. While the clay dish is drying, cut a traced stencil of the starfish. The stencil should just fit into the center half or one-third of the dish, so the size depends on the size dish you are making and the proportion of design that looks best.
4. Do not let the clay stay on the saucer too long as it will shrink and make removal difficult. Just before removing, add a roll or strip of clay in the middle of the bottom as a supporting "foot."
5. When you have removed the clay dish shape, turn it upright. Place the stencil in the middle and start building up the cut-out starfish design with several layers of slip, adding the material with a brush and letting the slip dry between applications.
6. When the starfish design is whatever height you want it to be, remove the stencil and let the clay dish dry. Smooth out any rough areas with a wet sponge.
7. When thoroughly dry, bake in the kitchen oven. When cool, cover with the glaze color of your choice and let dry until hard.

FIG. 169. *Making the stencilled dish from clay.*

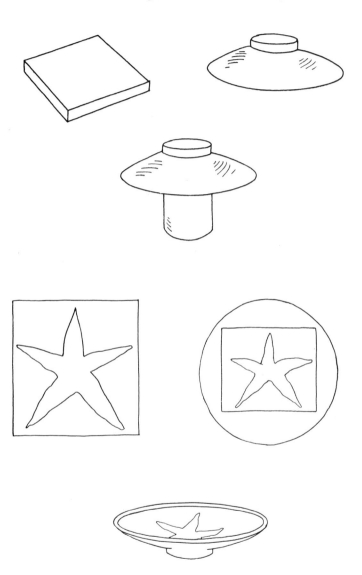

FIG. 170. *A Scallop Shell* (Pecten).

A JAR OF ANCIENT SHAPE

This circular shape with its straight sides, curved top and small opening looks like a salt-glazed jug or an old Chinese or Japanese form. It is decorated with a frieze of pressed clay Scallop Shells, and is classic in feeling.

Tools and Materials

For the plaster of Paris mold you will need a spoon, measuring cup, and a plastic mixing bowl or container. Materials needed are: plaster of Paris, mold box of cardboard, wood or plastic, and a large Scallop Shell (*Pecten*).

For the clay work, the tools are a rolling pin, two 15-inch-long pieces of wood lath ½ inch thick, a pointed paring knife, small sponge, a small plastic container for mixing and holding slip, assorted brushes, stirrers and mixing containers for the glazes, and a baking sheet.

The materials include oven-baking clay, air-dried glazes, as well as a small china or plastic bowl and a tin can—both the same circumference. A plastic cleaner's bag. Reread pages 219 and 220.

Steps

1. Make the plaster of Paris negative mold with the Scallop Shell.
2. Roll out a ½-inch-thick slab of clay.
3. Decide on the height of your jar. Wrap a length of clay around a large tin can and fasten the ends together with slip.

4. Drape another length of clay over the outside of your bowl and cut out a small circle of clay in the center. Trim off the bottom edges so they are even.

5. Cut a circle of clay the same size as the bottom of the can plus the thickness of the cylinder wall.

6. Press clay into the individual shells of the plaster of Paris shell mold. Make enough scallop castings to go around the bottom of the cylinder.

7. Let the pieces on the can and bowl dry until they are stiff enough to handle, but not too long, as they will shrink and cling tighter to the thin molds.

8. Take clay off the can and bowl. With slip, add the cylinder to the bottom circle. Then also using slip, add the shell forms around the bottom edge in a vertical position, the flat hinge area ½-inch above the bottom. Now add the upturned bowl shape, fitting it on the top edge of the cylinder with slip. Smooth the inside of the opening and add a thin roll of clay around the top edge as a finish.

9. Let dry, smooth with a damp sponge and bake.

10. Glaze with a gray glaze to which a little blue has been added. You can streak it a bit to look like a salt-glaze. Glaze the shells in a dark but lively blue. And then let the glaze dry until hard. Let them air-dry for several days; the results are worth the time.

Variation

Make only the lower half of the design, adding a rope of clay around the top. Overlap the shells in a running pattern. Glaze the background in off-white and the shells and rope in yellow, or the rope in blue for a Mediterranean look.

FIG. 171. (*Here and on following page*)

a. Models—bowl and can.

Fig. 171.
(continued)

b. *Plaster of Paris negative mold
(Step 1).*

c. *Wrapping clay slab around can
and draping clay over bowl
(Step 3 to 5).*

e. *Adding cylinder of clay
to bottom circle of clay
(Step 8).*

d. *Cast clay shells
(Step 6).*

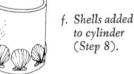

f. *Shells added
to cylinder
(Step 8).*

g. *Top "bowl" of clay
added to bottom
cylinder
(Step 8).*

h. *Bottom cylinder only
with a twist of clay
to finish the top
(variation).*

i. *Finished container.*

FIG. 172. *Sand dollar.*

A SILVER SAND DOLLAR

A sand dollar, cast in silvery resin, hangs around the neck on a silver chain—and a rubber mold makes it all possible.

Tools and Materials

Medium water-color brush, stirrer, small plastic measuring cup, and small plastic mixing container.

Rubber mold material, liquid casting resin and hardener, mold-release and aluminum powder. Sand dollar or keyhole urchin about 2 inches across (a *Mellita, Echinarachnius, Dendraster,* or *Lovenia*—depending on where along the east or west coast the sea urchin lives). Silver chain and a jump ring.

Steps

1. Make rubber mold in the shape of the sand dollar. (See page 212.)

2. Mix pouring resin and add a small quantity of aluminum powder. You will have to guess at the amount of powder as this depends on the type of pouring resin and the quantity of liquid you are using. Try a test piece first, making a record of the proportions used.

3. Fill the sand dollar rubber mold with only one pouring.

4. When hard, remove the casting from the mold.

5. Drill a tiny hole at the top of the sand dollar, or make the hole with a very thin hot nail or thick needle. If you have used a keyhole urchin, then the hole is already made. Add an oval jump ring and string the pendant on a silver chain.

Fig. 173. *The finished metallic-looking pendant.*

Variations

Use bronze powder instead of aluminum to give the pendant a gold tone.

You can also make a mold of a small starfish, sea horse, or a short piece of bladder-type seaweed known as Rockweed or Popping Wrack (*Fucus furcatus*).

Instead of casting resin and aluminum powder, fill the mold with liquid solder for a metal-like casting.

Fig. 174. *Small sea urchins.*

METALLIC SEA URCHINS

Instead of papery thin sea urchins which can easily crumble, make a metal casting that is permanent.

Tools and Materials

Medium water-color brush, stirrer, palette knife or small knife.

Rubber mold material, liquid solder or metal. Small 1- to 2-inch Sea Urchins (*Diadema antillarum, Strongylocentrotus dröbachiensis, Strongylocentrotus purpuratus*).

Steps

1. Start with a small sea urchin and make a rubber mold. First fasten a round of paper to the inside of the urchin to cover the top opening. Only cover the sides of the urchin with rubber-mold material to just under the bottom curve, not across the full bottom. (See page 212.)

2. Remove mold but be prepared for the possible breaking-up of the sea urchin as it is very fragile.

3. Fill the mold with liquid metal solder. Experiment with this process, following the manufacturer's general directions. You may want to cast in layers, allowing the first one to set before adding more material. Or, you may squeeze out a thin wall of solder around the whole inside of

241

the mold, letting this harden before filling in the middle. Or, if you fill the whole mold at one time, leave an open center core to help in drying the material evenly.

4. When hard, remove mold.

5. You can make several castings and arrange the sea urchins on a wooden block or on a slab of clear resin, holding them in position with epoxy cement.

Variation

Try making a rubber mold of a small Apple Murex (*Murex pomum*) or a Hairy Triton (*Cymatium aquitile*).

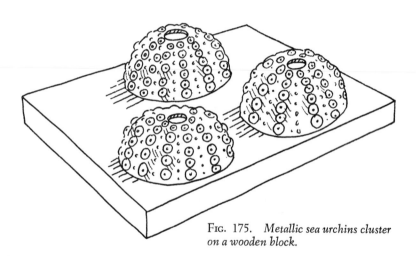

Fig. 175. *Metallic sea urchins cluster on a wooden block.*

PART III

SHELLS
AS
DESIGNS

7

Shell Printing with Crayons and Linoleum Blocks

HISTORICALLY, the hand-printing of fabrics and paper has been done with wood blocks. A far easier craft method is to use linoleum blocks which are available at all art stores. They are lightweight, wood-composition blocks with a ⅛-inch surface of linoleum painted white. The linoleum is easy to cut away with simple craft tools, and the white surface takes the carbon paper transfer of your design, making a clean, easy-to-see line for you to follow. The linoleum surface is also a good, smooth, inking area with no wood grain to interfere with your design.

A new process of craft fabric printing has been recently developed and the designs are almost interchangeable between the two techniques, even though the method of color application is quite different. In this second process, the designs are developed directly on paper, using a specially formulated colored crayon which is then made permanent on cloth by the application of a hot iron. A detailed description is given in this chapter. You will also find several projects described here with shells as a design inspiration.

TOOLS FOR LINOLEUM BLOCK CUTTING

One needs very few tools for linoleum block cutting and printing. Everything can be bought at an art store or any other shop selling art or craft supplies or by mail order. Look in the Yellow Pages of the telephone book for these stores.

You will need sharp cutting tools and the best are *X-acto knives*. The knife blades are made in several sizes and shapes, more or less wedge-shaped with a sharp point on one side; one handle fits several blade sizes. *Speedball linoleum cutters* or *blade gouges*, which are used in wood block cutting, are excellent for digging out chunks of linoleum from the interior part of a design.

A *brayer or roller* which has a rubber cylinder, 4 inches long and 1 inch in diameter, moves freely on heavy bent wire which also forms the handle. This is used to rub the cloth or paper against the inked block or sometimes to apply ink to a block. A large *tablespoon* is often used to rub over the paper, transferring the ink from the block.

Palette knife or a small *thin spatula* is necessary for mixing the ink and applying ink to dabber. The usual assortment of *ruler, pencil, scissors* and *eraser*.

FIG. 176. *Block printing tools, clockwise: broad cutting knife, narrow scoop knife, two cutting blades, handle for cutting blades and narrow cutting knife. In the center: two linoleum blocks.*

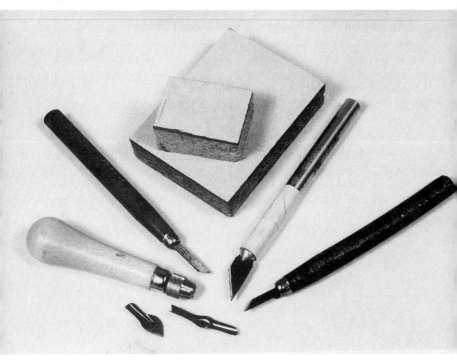

MATERIALS FOR LINOLEUM BLOCK CUTTING AND PRINTING

Linoleum blocks are sold in many sizes. If you cannot find the exact size you need, buy a slightly larger size and cut it down with a saw. This is very easy to do as the wood backing is soft.

Block printing ink is manufactured as both *oil-based ink* and *water-based ink*. The oil base is best for fabrics that you intend to wash. The water-based ink is quick-drying and ideal for paper printing. Tools and hands are cleaned quickly with water, while the oil-base variety needs *turpentine* for a cleaner and thinner.

Turpentine as a cleaner and thinner for oil-based ink. Also a *dryer* to speed up the drying time of the ink.

Fabrics for wall hangings, placemats, curtains, towels, pillows can be any plain or solid color material you wish to use.

Paper napkins, towels, notepaper, cards, special art papers for framable prints—all can be your own choice of texture and color.

Tracing paper or *onion skin typewriter paper* for tracing designs.

Carbon paper for transferring designs to the linoleum blocks.

General supplies are *clear food wrap, absorbent cotton, plastic coffee can tops,* and lots of *newspapers* for the working surface and drying area.

DEVELOPING A DESIGN

For both block printing and crayon printing, a bold simple design is the most effective. A block-printed design will appear as flat masses of color. Fine, raised lines are hard to cut and are liable to break while you are cutting if you are not familiar with the methods and tools.

There are several ways of working out your design. First, choose a shell of recognizable shape—a cone, bonnet, scallop, starfish, murex, spider—to name only a few. If you do not have one of these shells, find a picture in this book, a handbook or the encyclopedia and, using a soft pencil on tracing paper, make an exact copy of the outline. If you have a shell, lay it on a piece of tracing paper and trace around the outline. This will give you a solid-color silhouette design—the simplest one of all to cut and print. If either method of tracing produces a design too small or too large for your project, then enlarge or reduce the tracing, following the method given in the next section.

You can add detail to this flat design by *scooping* out a thin line which will then appear as the background color of your paper or cloth. For a

Cone Shell, a few curved lines at the top will emphasize the pointed design. The ray pattern on the Scallop Shell, the interior design on the arms of a starfish, all add interest to the finished printing.

Now to go one step further. Some of the Japanese Cone Shells, or the South Pacific area bonnet type, have designs that look like oriental fabrics. Both the shells and the block print designs are shown in Figs. 193 and 194. Notice that the bold geometric shapes follow the curve of the shell, giving your design a three-dimensional look. If you want to be really authentic, use a dark brown ink as both shells are brown and creamy white.

You will notice that all the printed portions—the raised areas of your block—are simple, massive shapes. In the silhouette shapes, the whole shell area is raised and the fine lines are dug out of the linoleum so there is no chance of fine lines breaking.

ENLARGING OR REDUCING A DESIGN

Both enlarging and reducing a design can be done by the same method. The first step is to "square-off" the design. Depending on its size, measure off horizontal and vertical lines to form squares in a grid over the whole drawing area. These squares can be anywhere from ⅛ to ½ inch, depending on the size of the original drawing. The lines can be drawn directly over the design, or on a separate sheet of tracing paper.

On a second sheet of tracing paper, draw the outline of the grid to the size of your final drawing. Measure off even squares, horizontally and vertically—*the same number of squares as you made on your design.*

Now copy the original design, following the lines as they cross the squares and intersect the lines. In this way you will end up with an exact reproduction of your original, either larger or smaller.

TRANSFERRING THE DESIGN

Once the final design has been drawn to size on a piece of tracing paper, you are ready to transfer it to the whitened surface of the linoleum block. In all cases, the tracing paper should be placed *face down* with the pencil lines against the block, so that, in the final printing, the design will be facing the right way. All shells have left and right sides and to reverse the design spoils the effect. This is especially important if you are including any lettering in your design—names or initials.

You have your choice of three methods of transferring the design. As you will be able to see the pencil lines on the "right side" through the

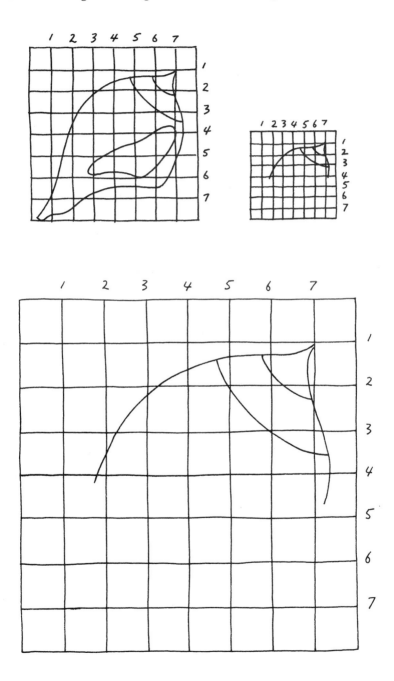

FIG. 177. Diagram showing the reduction and enlargement of a drawing.

thin tracing paper, the simplest way is to follow the pencil lines with either a hard pencil point or ballpoint pen. The pressure will transfer your original pencil lines on the right side to the block. As this will be a rather light line and easily smudged, this way is best used for a simple outline of a silhouetted shell. The second method is to cover a separate small piece of paper with soft-pencil lines, going back and forth until you have a solid black tone. Put the blackened side against the block, then put the reversed design on top and draw around the outlines seen through the tracing paper. The third and best is to use a good black carbon paper, placing the carbon side against the block and your reversed drawing on top. This line will not rub off in working and this method is particularly good if you have small and careful details to follow.

CUTTING THE LINOLEUM BLOCK

First, protect your working surface with several thicknesses of newspaper in case your cutting tools should slip. Always cut the block away from you. When you are cutting the background of a design, cut toward the edge of the block so if your tool slips, you will not gouge and spoil a center design. Remember that anything to be inked and printed is raised from the surface (see Fig. 179).

You will be using a combination of a sharp cutting knife and concave blade scoop knives. Take off small pieces of the linoleum at a time, starting at the edge and working back toward your design. Leave a very thin layer of linoleum over the wood as an anchor for the center design. As you get near the outline, cut part way down into the surface with the pointed end of the knife as this will protect your design from any chance of a piece of linoleum chipping off the printing surface.

Continue to work around your design until all the excess material is removed and there are no high points in the background that will catch the ink. Be careful also, not to undercut the outline, instead try for a slightly outward slope to the edge. If your shell design is a pure silhouette, then your work is done. If not, using knife and gougers, take out the necessary material on the inside of your design. You will find that you do not have to dig down quite so deeply as you did for the outside area.

Once the design is cut, you are ready to print—that is all there is to it.

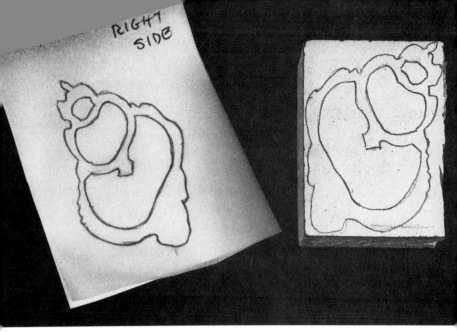

Fig. 178.   *Fossil shell design transferred to linoleum block. (See Fig. 184 for photograph of fossil shell.)*

Fig. 179.   *Cutting out the design.*

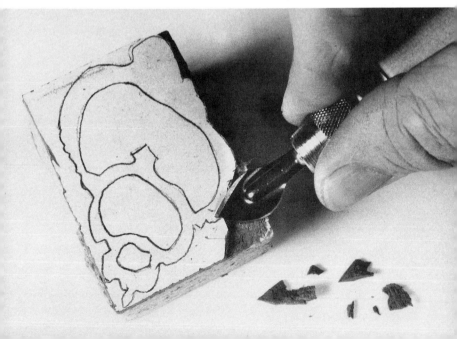

PREPARING YOUR WORKING SURFACE FOR PRINTING

Plan to do your printing in a non-traffic area as your printed paper or cloth will have to be laid out flat to dry undisturbed—perhaps for 24 hours. Put newspapers over the floor as a drying area and cover printing area with several layers of newspaper.

To make a dabber for applying ink to the block, cut a 2-inch square of absorbent cotton. Place it on a piece of clear plastic wrap. Bring the wrap up and around the cotton and tie it at the top with a string or a paper-covered wire twistum. Cut off all but 2 inches of the excess wrap above the tied area. Press down a bit so the dabber is flat on the bottom. Before plastic, block printers used oiled silk for this purpose.

For repeated printings of cards, notepaper or party napkins, a design is placed in the same position by using a styrofoam sheet to hold the block. This is particularly true of a large block print which is too big for your hand to place accurately on the paper or cloth, and too large also for a quick downward pressure to form a good print.

The sheet of styrofoam should be larger than your block and the same thickness as the wood (on the block) or slightly less, as the printing surface should be above the styrofoam level. Cut an opening in the styrofoam to just fit the block. Also be sure the sheet of styrofoam is large enough to give your paper some support. Try the block and paper placement before cutting to make sure the block is in the best area of the sheet. After cutting the styrofoam, fit the block into the opening, face side up. With a ruler and felt-tipped pen, mark off the guide lines for your paper or cloth.

Have one or two paper towels handy and a small bowl of water or turpentine to clean ink drips from the block.

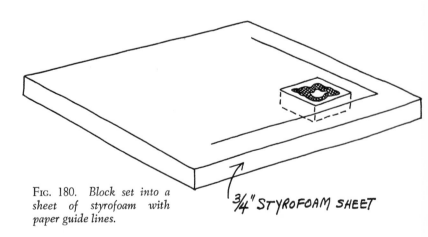

Fig. 180. *Block set into a sheet of styrofoam with paper guide lines.*

¾" STYROFOAM SHEET

MIXING THE INK

Block printing inks made by several manufacturers can be bought in most art stores or art supply departments. There are two varieties: one is an oil-based ink which can be used on both fabric and paper; the other is a water-soluble ink which is for paper printing only.

The range of colors is limited in comparison to the colors available in tubes of regular oil or water-color paint. The primary and secondary colors plus brown, white and black are all there, with a variation or two of each color. However, like any tube paint, the colors can be mixed with each other—water ink with water ink, oil ink with oil ink only—to form individual shades and tones.

A flat, non-absorbent surface is best for mixing the inks. You can use the round plastic tops from coffee cans, shallow aluminum foil pans from freezer products, or a piece of glass.

Squeeze out a small amount of ink at a time, 1 to 2 inches, as you will be surprised how far it goes in printing. If you are mixing colors, make a note by measurement of how much ink from each tube you used so that you can match the color again—for instance 1 inch of red and ½ inch of blue to make a reddish purple. Do not use too large a container and keep the ink within as small an area as you can. Smooth and blend it with the palette knife or any blunt-ended knife, adding a little water or turpentine (depending on the ink you are using), until the ink is still thick but not gummy. Add a drop or two of drier to the oil-based ink.

You are now ready to apply ink to the block.

FIG. 181. *Block printing inks and supplies, clockwise from top: rubber roller, printing inks, palette knife, ink on plastic coffee can top, dabber and tube of ink.*

PRINTING THE BLOCK

Your block is cut, ink is ready, working surface prepared and the drying area waiting for the first printed project.

Place a small amount of ink on your dabber with the end of the palette knife. Smooth it over an area about the size of a quarter. Dab away at your design on the top of the block, covering it with a thin layer of ink. Now press the block down on your test paper or fabric, rock the block firmly in position and lift up sharply.

Study the print carefully. Is the image clear? Too little, or too much ink? Have any high spots on the background picked up ink? Is the ink too thick or too thin? Correct any faults and print several more images to perfect your printing technique and to "break in" the printing block.

Now begin your real printing. Work carefully, making each print the best one you can do. Put prints on the floor to dry. They should be left undisturbed for 24 hours to be sure the ink is thoroughly dry.

Another way to apply the ink is to use the roller. The ink should be mixed on a flat piece of glass. The roller is run over the ink surface until it is covered with a thin coat of ink. Then the ink is rolled over the block, covering the surface. After placing the block on the paper, lift up sharply.

Put a large block in a sheet of styrofoam (see Fig. 180). Ink the block by dabbing, place the paper over the block, following your guidelines, and go over the paper two or three times with a clean roller or brayer, bracing the paper firmly so it will not move and so cause smudging of the print. Using both hands, lift up the paper quickly and cleanly.

Large blocks can also be inked with a roller that has been run over an ink-covered sheet of glass. The paper is put over the inked block, and a clean roller used to press the paper evenly against the block. You can also rub the paper against the block surface with the back of a large metal tablespoon.

After a number of printings, the block begins to get sticky as the ink piles up on the surface. Using a clean paper towel and either water or turpentine depending on your ink, wipe off the surface. If the block is set into the styrofoam sheet, take it out before washing as you do not want to smear the styrofoam surface. A messy styrofoam would mess up your printing paper.

If you want an overall design or a repeat border using more than one color, plan your areas carefully and print all the designs in one color. Then, thoroughly wash off your block to remove any vestiges of color. Mix up the second color and print all the areas where this color will appear. If further colors are planned, follow the washing, mixing and printing procedures.

Now turn to the projects in this chapter. You will use these techniques in all of them, as described in the step-by-step procedures.

CRAYON PRINTING

This is a colorful process which allows for a great deal of free-hand drawing; it is best suited to cloth printing. However, it is a one-time printing design, unless you make a stencil from lightweight bristol board.

Crayon printing is a transfer process, similar to block printing, except that the "printing" base is a sheet of paper on which the design is made with special crayons of one or several colors. This sheet is laid face down on the cloth, and heat is applied to the back to effect the transfer. This means that your crayon drawing has to be made in reverse of the final printed effect—in the same way as the cut linoleum block design.

Tools for Crayon Printing

An *electric iron* for transferring crayon color from paper drawing to the cloth. A *small stiff brush* for removing extra crayon crumbles from the paper pattern. A *ruler, pencil, scissors, X-acto knife* for cutting stencils.

Materials for Crayon Printing

Lightweight drawing paper, which is used for the original crayon drawing. *Tracing paper* for first sketches. Lightweight *bristol board* or *oiled paper* for stencils. *Fabric* of the synthetic variety such as dacron and polyester, rather than cotton. *Special crayons* for fabric printing (Crayola Craft Fabric Crayons). Lots of *newspaper.*

FIG. 182. *Fabric printing crayons and a test sample of colors.*

Developing a Design

Before beginning any design work, make a test run of the colors and the transfer technique. Make squares of each color in varying intensities and patterns of solid color and shading, and in as many variations as you think you might use. In fact, make two sheets as near alike as you can. One to transfer, the other to keep untransferred as a comparison. This will give you almost foolproof guidance as you work on your final projects. (Instructions on how to transfer the color pattern are given in the next section.) Now that you have made your test sheets proceed with the final designs.

In working with colored crayons, it is best to start with a simple, recognizable form. Thin outlines are not critical, and a certain amount of shading can be developed. Try working out a design which shows the cutaway interior of a shell. Shell catalogs contain photographs of "slices" of murex, nautilus and several other species. Make tracings or free-hand copies to be transferred.

First make a small rough color sketch of your idea. When it is just the way you want it, enlarge or reduce the design following the directions on page 248. Make the final pencil outline on tracing paper. Turn the paper over and *lightly* transfer this pattern to the final drawing paper. You do not want a heavy lead pencil line as this will interfere with the action of the crayon.

Fill in with the color or colors you have chosen, checking with your two test sheets so that you will know the final results.

For a repeat drawing, as an overall fabric design for a pillow, a border, a hanging, or even a set of matching placemats, you can re-use your tracing-paper design, replenishing the pencil outline on the "transfer" side.

A second method for a repeated pattern is to make a stencil. For this, your design will need to be a bold form that is easily cut out, with the interior of the form solid or shaded in the final drawing. You can even make a feature of the stencil effect by making an overlapping design of shells, each one separated by a broad line of stencil paper. Or, cut narrow outlines and interior pattern in the stencil paper to form a graphic design.

For the stencil, choose a lightweight bristol board, thin enough to cut with scissors, X-acto, or razor knife, yet stiff enough to stay flat and not crumple during several uses. Make your drawing on tracing paper first, turn over and transfer to the bristol board. Remember, everything you cut out will be color, everything left uncut will be the cloth background or the area you will fill in with crayon. Mark the face of the stencil for

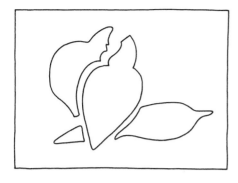

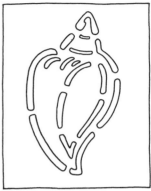

Fig. 183. *Drawing shows two approaches to cutting a stencil design.*

right side up. You can always flip the stencil over in a repeated pattern to give variation to the design.

Put the stencil down on the drawing paper and hold lightly in place with a short piece of masking tape on each side. Fill in the exposed areas with crayons. Lift up the stencil, and make any finishing adjustments or additions. You can achieve a block-printing effect of solid unshaded color with this reproduction method.

Whatever method you use, set the drawing aside while you prepare the transfer surface.

Transferring the Color Pattern

Depending on the size of your design, you can either do the transferring on an ironing board or on a well-protected table.

Whichever procedure you are using, cover the surface with a number of sheets of newspaper, finishing up with a clean sheet of white drawing paper. Place the fabric over the paper, smoothing it out so there are no wrinkles. Have some idea of just where on the cloth your design is going to be printed. Stick pins upright into the surface and through the padding where the four corners of the pattern paper will rest.

Before placing the crayon drawing face down on the cloth, check for any stray crayon crumbles and brush them off with a small, stiff paint brush.

257

Now put the crayon drawing in place, face down on the cloth. Cover with a second sheet of clean, white drawing paper. This will act as an absorbent sheet, keeping any crayon from the bottom of the iron.

Heat the iron to a strong heat—cotton setting is best. Press down firmly but evenly on the iron as you run it back and forth over the entire surface. Be careful not to move the print or crumple the surface of the protecting paper. Lift up a corner of the design to see how well the transferring is progressing and if the fabric is standing up to the heat without turning color. When the crayon color has seeped through faintly to the top sheet of paper, your transfer is complete.

Peel off both sheets of paper very carefully, peeking under to make sure the design is properly transferred. If not, let paper fall back into place and run the iron over the critical spot again, pressing down firmly.

Your project is now finished, and the color will remain on the fabric permanently and be completely washable.

PRINTED PARTY PAPERS

A center slice of a Snail Shell is the basic design for a block-printing design to be used on cocktail or luncheon size paper napkins and on throwaway guest towels. For your design look in a shell identification handbook, a shell supplier's catalog or the encyclopedia for drawings or photographs of a cross-section of Gastropods or Snail Shells. Or copy the design shown here in Fig. 184. This is a small ⅜-inch-long fossilized Nassarius Shell of the Pliocene period, which was embedded in a rock long, long ago. It was worn down by the sea until just its skeleton shows whitely in the center of the light tan pebble that I found on a stony beach on the southwest coast of Puerto Rico.

FIG. 184. *Fossil shell in a pebble.*

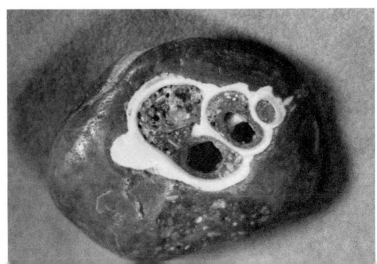

Tools and Materials

You will need X-acto or Speedball linoleum block cutters, a brayer or roller, palette knife, an ink dabber, and the usual assortment of ruler, pencil and scissors.

Linoleum block, water-soluble ink, plastic top from coffee can, flat piece of ¾-inch-thick styrofoam, tracing paper, paper napkins, paper guest towels and notepaper.

Steps

1. Make a drawing on tracing paper of your design, enlarging or reducing shell picture to fit block area of 1½ x 2 inches. (See page 249.)

2. Transfer drawing to block, placing tracing paper face down.

3. Cut out design. (See page 250.)

4. Make dabber, mix ink and cover working and drying surfaces with newspaper.

5. Open out napkins or guest towels so that you will be printing on only one thickness, or the ink will soak through the other layers.

6. Decide on the placement of your design: angled up from one corner, with the broadest point in the corner; or, two shell prints side by side, but in reverse direction, again pointing up from the free lower corner toward the folded section. For guest towels: straight across the bottom; in the middle of the towel in a vertical position; several designs scattered helter-skelter over the surface; all in one color or in two colors.

7. Make a few test printings to check on the amount of ink needed and the pressure to exert on the block.

8. Start your final printing. You will find that each shell print may be at a slightly different angle and that the intensity of the ink will vary, but that is the beauty of a hand-crafted product. (Fig. 185.)

9. Let dry for 24 hours.

Variation

A block-printed shell in the corner of a sheet of notepaper proclaims that the writer is an individualist. So use the fossil shell block, or cut a different one—a Royal Comb Venus Shell (*Pitar dione*), for instance.

Additionally, have a rubber stamp made, picking an interesting type face for your name and address, or just your name. Add this to your design as a separate printing, using the same ink.

PLACEMATS

Print a single design in the corner of a neutral or brightly colored fabric to create placemats that are all yours. A clever variation is to print on fine, split bamboo or woven palm-leaf mats. All of these make great gifts for friends. (Fig. 189.)

Tools and Materials

An X-acto or Speedball linoleum block cutter, a brayer or roller, palette knife, an ink dabber, and the usual assortment of ruler, pencil and scissors.

Depending on the placemat project, you will need a heavy cotton, linen or synthetic plain fabric, either as yard goods or manufactured solid-color placemats. Straw, or fine split-bamboo mats, or plain paper mats. Waterproof printing ink and a linoleum block of the right size for your project. If you are printing on throwaway paper mats, then use a water-based ink.

Steps

1. If you have bought a length of material, measure, cut and then hem the placemats.

2. Make the shell design, transfer it to the block and cut out. As a design, try one of the Spider Shells (*Lambis*), the round skeleton of a Sea Urchin (*Strongylocentrotus* or *Diadema*), or one of the many species of starfish, or a sea biscuit which is a form of Caribbean Sand Dollar.

3. Print the material. The design can be a single large Spider Shell at the top right-hand side of the mat or two large sea urchins across the top. Try printing one block, then a second printing of the same block just overlapping the first one—both in the same color or in two different colors.

Variations

Use split-bamboo mats bought in a Japanese gift shop; or woven straw mats instead of cloth. Proceed as you did with the cloth mats.

A single Cone Shell block can be repeated as a stripe on each side of the mat.

Throwaway paper mats can be printed in quantity.

SPLIT BAMBOO SHADES

This project is really an extension of the placemat designs except that here we print on matchstick-bamboo window shades. Make large, bold forms as you will be printing on a larger surface. Roughly sketch out the placement of the block designs on a proportionately smaller sheet of paper and follow it for the placement of your prints. The design may be one of a random placement of shells over the whole surface, or a straight band carried across the width of the shade at several levels.

Whatever the design, stretch the shade out flat on the floor over several thickness of newspaper before printing and let dry without disturbing after the printing.

BLOCK-PRINTED WALL HANGING

A very striking, small modern wall hanging is made from a cut-away shell design, printed in dark, vibrant blue against a red cloth, with a bamboo pole through the top and bottom hem.

Tools and Materials

An X-acto or Speedball linoleum block cutter, a brayer or roller, palette knife, an ink dabber, and the usual assortment of ruler, pencil and scissors.

Heavy butcher linen or canvas cloth in a deep but bright red, approximately 19 x 19 inches. Block print, tracing paper, and washable ink in a royal blue color. Two bamboo poles, 17 inches long. A length of cord for hanging.

Steps

1. The top and bottom hems will be approximately 1 inch deep to allow for the thickness of the bamboo poles, which should fit snugly into the hem. Trim sides to allow for a ¼- to ½-inch hem, keeping a 15 x 15-inch finished proportion for the hanging. Machine-stitch all around.

2. The design is a repetition of a cut-away shell and a thick "comma." The shells angle in from each corner with the pointed ends almost touching in the center. The thick commas fill in the four spaces between the shells, as in Fig. 191. The whole design is made to fill a 12-inch-square area.

3. Make a rough drawing to size so that you will have the right proportion of shell and comma. Finish one shell and one comma and trace onto thin paper.

4. Transfer the drawings to two blocks and cut out.

5. Mix color and test the design on paper cut to the finished size of your hanging.

6. Make the final print on the cloth and let dry.

7. Notch around one pole, ½-inch in from each end. Slip into the top hem of the wall hanging. Tie each end of the cord onto the pole, settling the cord into the notches. Slip the other pole into the bottom of the hanging and your project is complete.

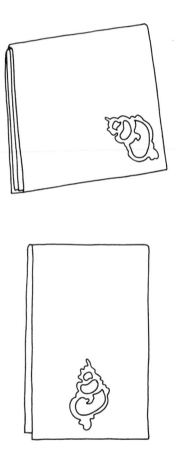

FIG. 185.   *Block design printed on paper napkins or towels (page 258).*

Fig. 186. *Royal Comb Venus* (Pitar dione).

Fig. 187. *Block print design on notepaper.*

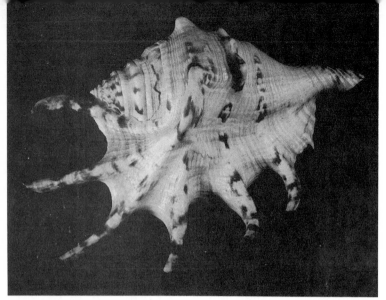

FIG. 188. *Spider Shell* (Lambis).

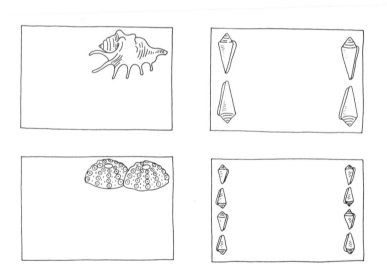

FIG. 189. *Various designs for placemats* (page 260).

264

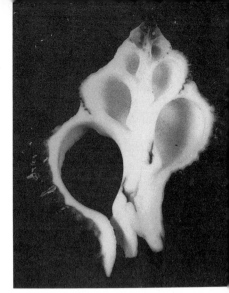

Fig. 190. *A sliced-through Murex Shell.*

Fig. 191. *Finished wall hanging design covering the full square of material (left), and variations (pages 261 and 266).*

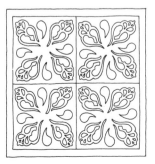

CRAYON-PRINTED WALL HANGING

This project is the same as the "Block-Printed Wall Hanging" (see previous section) so that the two techniques can be compared when the same design is involved.

Tools and Materials

The most minimum tools are needed. An electric iron, a small stiff brush, a ruler, pencil, scissors, and that's it.

A box of Crayola Craft Fabric Crayons, tracing paper, lightweight drawing paper, a 19- x 19-inch piece of red dacron polyester, two 17-inch-long bamboo poles, cord for hanging, plus lots of newspaper.

Steps

1. Cut and hem fabric according to directions given in "Block-Printed Wall Hanging" (Step 1).

2. Make a design layout to size. You might want to use a Murex Shell. Look in catalogs and shell books for cut-away designs. Make a final drawing of one shell plus a fat comma.

3. Trace the shell design onto the lightweight drawing paper, repeating the shell four times and the comma four times.

4. Fill in the design with dark blue crayon, making a solid, unshaded surface.

5. Transfer to the cloth.

6. Add the bamboo poles as described in Step 7, "Block-Printed Wall Hanging."

Variations

To make a scarf, print design in the center of a 24- or 32-inch square of light dacron polyester material. Perhaps an orange background with a bright green design. Experiment also in shading the design, rather than achieving a flat, solid color.

Follow the other suggestions given in Fig. 191.

Variation in either block or crayon printing

As a scarf. Plan on a 32-inch square scarf of lightweight, silky finished material. The design becomes four repeats of the 12-inch square, allowing for a 4-inch margin all around. Choose your favorite cloth color and contrasting ink and print away. Or, center the 12-inch square in the middle of the 32-inch square scarf. Or, border the scarf with alternating shell and comma, both with points facing inward.

You can also work out the use of two or more colors for printing with all of the above designs. So you can see that the effects are many and exciting.

As a pillow. Use the same design, or develop a flowing seaweed design, printed as a flat color silhouetted block; or use the shaded crayon technique. Shell block designs can be added. (Fig. 192.)

ALLOVER FABRIC DESIGN

Many Pacific Ocean Cones and Helmet Shells have fascinating patterns, looking like Japanese silks. These can be copied and cut into the blocks or made into crayon transfers for allover patterns on scarfs, pillows, wall hangings, or small designs on scarfs, and large blow-ups on pillows and wall hangings. The natural colors are brown and rust and ivory, but you can let your imagination take over for color combinations.

Tools and Materials

For block printing the tools needed are an X-acto or Speedball linoleum block cutter, a brayer or roller, palette knife, an ink dabber, and the usual assortment of ruler, pencil and scissors.

Linoleum block, washable ink, plastic top from coffee can, tracing paper, and cloth suitable for whatever project you are going to make.

For crayon printing you'll need an electric iron, a small stiff brush, a ruler, pencil and scissors.

The materials include Crayola Craft Fabric Crayons, tracing paper, lightweight drawing paper, dacron polyester fabric and lots of newspaper.

Steps

1. Find one of the Cone Shells from the Pacific in a shell shop, or look in a shell book for a photograph. The one shown here is *Cucullus bandanus* which is 3 inches long and brown and white in color. Others have jagged lines or dots, and some cones have brown-and-white patterns that look like dancing figures. (Fig. 193.)

2. Wrap a thin piece of tracing paper around the shell and, with a black ballpoint pen, trace the design; in this way you will be transferring the full-round design to a flat surface.

3. Using the tracing as your master design, either add extra triangles to square out the design or cut away some of the original drawing to make a square. Enlarge or reduce the squared pattern, depending on how you want to use it. Or, leave the pattern in its original fan shape.

4. If you are going to make a block print, then trace the design onto the white surface and cut the block.

5. Your pattern can be used as a border around a scarf, or to cover a whole piece of cloth by repeating the design over and over, either in the same position of the block or by turning the block around so that the pattern changes with each printing. Experiment on a sheet of paper of the same size as the material to be printed. This design can also be used for wall hangings. (Fig. 194.)

6. If you are printing with crayons, try blowing up the pattern or sections of the pattern to fit a 12-inch square or larger surface, depending on whether you want to fill the whole pillow square or leave a plain border around the center.

Variations

Try other shell designs. If you have cut a large shell block, or have a large shell tracing for crayon printing, try combining the allover pattern in a light color with the large shell superimposed in a dark vibrant color. As you make shell blocks or tracings for crayon printing in different sizes, you will find whole new projects combining the shells into new patterns.

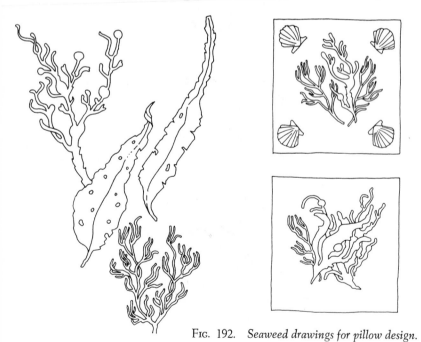

Fig. 192. *Seaweed drawings for pillow design.*

Fig. 193. *A small Conch Shell at the top and two Pacific cones with brown-and-white designs.*

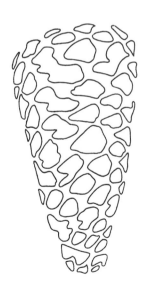

Fig. 194. *Cone pattern traced flat and suggested uses in printing.*

A TOTE BAG

This heavy canvas tote is bag and handle all in one, with a large printed shell front and back. Or, use a heavy dacron polyester fabric with a separate lining and print the design from a crayon transfer.

Tools and Materials

For block printing, the tools needed are an X-acto or Speedball linoleum block cutter, a brayer or roller, palette knife, an ink dabber, and the usual assortment of ruler, pencil and scissors.

Linoleum block, washable ink, plastic top from coffee can, tracing paper, and ½ yard of 36-inch-wide material if you are using heavy canvas. If a lighter weight, then buy 1 yard of 36-inch-wide material so that you can line the bag, or buy two ½-yards of contrasting material.

For crayon printing you'll need an electric iron, a small stiff brush, a ruler, pencil and scissors.

The materials include Crayola Craft Fabric Crayons, tracing paper, lightweight drawing paper, and dacron polyester fabric the same measurements as above, plus lots of newspaper.

The design is based on either a large Trumpet Shell (*Charonia tritonis nobilis*) or a *Cassis areola* from Australia.

Steps

1. Make a paper pattern of the tote bag. See Fig. 196 for measurements. Depending on your height and preference in a bag size, vary the measurements.

2. Cut out the bag and lining, if you are planning to have one.

3. Work out the size of your shell design on the pattern of the tote bag.

4. Trace shell pattern and transfer either to the block or to a sheet of stiff white paper for the crayon transfer process. Remember that you can make a large shell with the crayon process, adding shading and more than one color. For block printing you need a bolder outline and a simple inner pattern.

5. Print the design on both front and back of the unsewn bag.

6. When printing is complete and dry, turn under and hem the curved top and arm band. Next, sew side and bottom together. If you are lining the bag, first sew the side and bottom seams of the lining. Put the wrong sides of bag and lining together, turn under the hem of the top and arm band and sew the two thicknesses of material together on the outside.

Fɪɢ. 195.   Cassis areola.

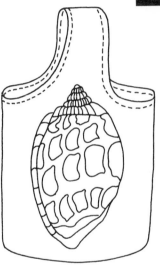

Fɪɢ. 196.   *Finished tote bag and pattern.*

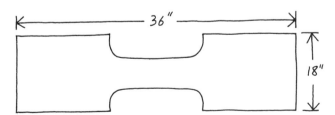

36"

18"

Variations

You can use one of these large designs for a scarf—two trumpets will fill one scarf square. (Fig. 198.)

Repeat the printing of a large shell around the bottom edge of a long skirt for an effective decoration.

The beauty of making a number of tracings and blocks is that they are interchangeable for all the printing projects and can be combined into many fantastic designs.

Fig. 197. *Trumpet Shell* (Charonia tritonis nobilis).

Fig. 198. *Trumpet scarf design.*

8

Final Word for Future Projects

You will find that all of the projects in this book are interchangeable—one technique can replace another, or be adapted to new projects—as all of the methods described are basic approaches to craft designs. Shells, too, can be substituted, depending on what species are available.

Large wall hangings can be made with intricate patterns of applied shells, using the same method as for straw bag decoration. Or, drilled shells can be sewn onto fabric as a wall hanging or onto straw placemats.

Commercial macramé plant hangers are made more personal with the addition of shells, or make your own macramé hangers or belts, or even a non-objective sculpture combining shells and fibers in a design to hang from ceiling to floor.

You will find endless fun with shells—first in gathering them on a beach or in searching out treasure in shell shops, then identifying them, and using the shells for decoration where they will be seen and enjoyed as a reminder of the original treasure hunt and proof of your own skill as a craftsperson.

Sources for Supplies

FOR RETAIL STORE SOURCES in your area look in the Yellow Pages of the telephone directory under the heading Arts and Crafts; Hobby and Model Construction Supplies; Jeweler's Supplies and Findings; Shells—Marine. Hardware stores and variety stores carry many of the supplies. There are many trademarked products similar to those described in the book so use what is available in your area.

Here is a listing of those companies that sell by mail order. Most supply a catalog, free unless otherwise indicated. Some retail stores are listed and these will be indicated as such.

Block and Crayon Printing

Binney & Smith, Inc.
1107 Broadway
New York, N.Y. 10001
(Crayola Craft Fabric Crayons. Write for name of local outlet.)

Dixon-The American Crayon Co.
Sandusky, Ohio 44870
(Prang Textile Colors. Write for name of local outlet.)

Hunt Manufacturing Co.
Statesville, N.C. 28677
(Speedball block printing knives, block printing ink—water-soluble and oil base. Write for name of local outlet.)

F. Weber
Philadelphia, Pa. 19144
(Block printing ink—water-soluble and oil base. Write for name of local outlet.)

X-acto, Inc.
48-41 Van Dam St.
Long Island City, N.Y. 11101
(Cutting knives)

Clay and Glazes

Sculpture House
30 East 30th St.
New York, N.Y. 10016
(Della Robbia Clay—oven-baked, and matching glazes)

Jewelry Findings, Metal and Supplies

Abbey Materials Corp.
245 West 29th St.
New York, N.Y. 10001

Alfa Products
Ventron Corp.
152 Andover St.
Danvers, Mass. 01923
(Catalog $1.00)

Allcraft
100 Frank Rd.
Hicksville, N.Y. 11801
(Mail order address)

Allcraft
45 West 46th St.
New York, N.Y. 10036
(Retail store)

American Handicrafts Co.
1001 Foch St.
Fort Worth, Tex. 76109
(Write for names of local stores.)

American Metalcraft, Inc.
4100 West Belmont Ave.
Chicago, Ill. 60641

ARE Creations Inc.
Box 155 E
Plainfield, Vt. 05667

Bergen Arts and Crafts
P. O. Box 381
Marblehead, Mass. 01945
(Catalog $1.00)

Brookstone Company
Brookstone Bldg.
Peterborough, N.H. 03458

Crown Manufacturing Co.
1188 Industrial Ave.
Escondido, Calif. 92882

Davis Crafts
86 West Old Wilson Bridge Rd.
Columbus, Ohio 43085
(No catalog)

Gemcraft of Wichita
300 N. Main
Wichita, Kan. 67202

Gems Galore
1328 El Camino Real
Mountain View, Calif. 94040
(Catalog 50¢)

Gilman's
Hellertown, Pa. 18055

The Globe
220 Albert St.
East Lansing, Mich. 48823

Grieger's
900 S. Arroyo Pkwy.
Pasadena, Calif. 95470

Lapidary Center
4114 Judah St.
San Francisco, Calif. 94122

Sheru
49 West 38th St.
New York, N.Y. 10018
(No catalog)

Shipley's Mineral House
Gem Village
Bayfield, Colo. 81122

Smokey Mountain Rock Shop
San Carlos Blvd.
Ft. Myers, Fla. 33902

C. W. Somers and Co.
387 Washington St.
Boston, Mass. 02108

Swest
10803 Composite Dr.
Dallas, Tex. 75220
(Catalogs 474 and F-72, $2.00 for set)

California Crafts Supply
Box 3277
Anaheim, Calif. 92882

TSI
487 Elliot Ave. West
Seattle, Wash. 98119
(Catalog $1.00)

Myron Toback Inc.
23 West 47th St.
New York, N.Y. 10036

U.S. Lapidary Supply Co.
1605 West San Carlos St.
San Jose, Calif. 95128

C. Weidinger
4404 Del Prado Pkwy.
P. O. Box 5
Cape Coral, Fla. 33904

X-acto, Inc.
48-41 Van Dam St.
Long Island City, N.Y. 11101

Resin and Commercial Molds

Fibre Glass—Evercoat Products
6600 Cornell Road
Cincinnati, Ohio 45242
(Procoat—clear varnish resin, a water-proof sealer, and Crystal Clear—liquid polyester resin. Write for name of local store.)

Fry Plastics International, Inc.
10552 Trask Ave.
Garden Grove, Calif. 92643
(Crystal "Crystletts"—cooking crystals)

Quincrafts Corporation
542 East Squantum St.
Quincy, Mass. 02171
(Makit & Bakit—plastic cooking crystals)

Specialty Products
731 Brooks Road
Muskegon, Mich. 49442
(Liquid casting plastic [resin], "3-D" molds, Cookin' Crystals)

Rubber Mold Material

Sculpture House
30 East 30th St.
New York, N.Y. 10016
(Pliatex Mold Rubber)

Shells

(Many of the firms in this list also carry jewelry tools and supplies.)

Anozira
Box 3988
Tucson, Ariz. 85717

Bauer's
2126 45th St.
Galveston, Tex. 77750.

Benson's Import Co.
22 East Pacific Coast Hgwy.
Long Beach, Calif. 90806
(Retail store sales)

Buried Treasure, Inc.
12124 Nebel St.
Rockville, Md. 20852

Collectors Cabinet, The
153 East 57th St.
New York, N.Y. 10022

Crosby Gardens Rock and Shell Shop
5473 Shore Dr.
Virginia Beach, Va. 23455

Earth Products
14 Jackson Ave.
Peabody, Mass. 01960

Hollingsworth, Herman W.
U. S. 92
Box 338
Mango, Fla. 33550
(All shells, good catalog)

Kirk's Rock and Shell Shop
2037 University Blvd.
North Jacksonville, Fla. 32211

Wayne Kishbaugh
P. O. Box 1856
El Cajon, Calif. 92020
(Hishi, Puka)

Maxilla & Mandible Ltd.
451 Columbus Ave.
New York, N.Y. 10024

Reference Books

CARIBBEAN SEASHELLS by Germaine L. Warmke, M. S., and R. Tucker Abbot, Ph.D. Dover Publications, Inc., New York, N.Y., 1975

COLOURED ILLUSTRATIONS OF THE SHELLS OF JAPAN by Tetsuaki Kira, Hoikusha, Osaka, Japan, 1955

A FIELD GUIDE TO THE SHELLS (Atlantic and Gulf Coasts) by Percy A. Morris, Houghton Mifflin Company, Boston, Mass., 1950

A FIELD GUIDE TO SHELLS OF THE PACIFIC COAST AND HAWAII by Percy A. Morris, Houghton Mifflin Company, Boston, Mass., 1966

MARINE SHELLS OF THE WESTERN COAST OF FLORIDA by Louise M. Perry and Jeanne S. Schwengel, Paleontological Research Institution, Ithaca, N.Y., 1955

PLIOCENE MOLLUSCA OF SOUTHERN FLORIDA by Axel A. Olssen and Anne Harbison, The Academy of Natural Sciences of Philadelphia, Pa., 1953

TIDE POOLS AND BEACHES by Elizabeth Clemons, Alfred A. Knopf, New York, N.Y., 1964

Index